The Natural and Other Histories of
BATU CAVES

Text and photographs by
Shaharin Yussof

Published by the
Malaysian Nature Society.

Published by
THE MALAYSIAN NATURE SOCIETY
(PERSATUAN PENCINTA ALAM MALAYSIA)
P.O. Box 10750
50724 Kuala Lumpur
Malaysia.

Text copyright © 1997 Shaharin Yussof and The Malaysian Nature Society
Photographs copyright © 1997 Shaharin Yussof

All rights reserved.

No part of this book may be reproduced or transmitted,
in any form or by any means, electronic or mechanical,
including photocopying, recording,
or by any information storage retrieval system,
without prior permission from both copyright holders.

First Edition

ISBN 983 9681 04 4

Printed by United Selangor Press Sdn. Bhd.
No. 8 & 10 Jalan Lengkongan Brunei, Pudu
55100 Kuala Lumpur
Malaysia

DEDICATION

This book is dedicated to the memory of

Dr. Tho Yow Pong,

without whose enthusiasm and efforts,
as Secretary of the Malaysian Nature Society,
many of the Society's projects, including this one,
would never even have begun.

**WITH SPONSORSHIP ASSISTANCE
MADE AVAILABLE THROUGH
ROTARY CLUB OF GOMBAK
FROM**

FARID ASSOCIATES GROUP
Solution Providers

  kajCOMM

Corporate Office :
57-2, Medan Setia 1, Plaza Damansara, Bukit Damansara, 50490 Kuala Lumpur, Malaysia.
Tel : 03-254 3322, 255 5121, 254 6670, 252 1899, 254 7221 Fax : 03-256 2798

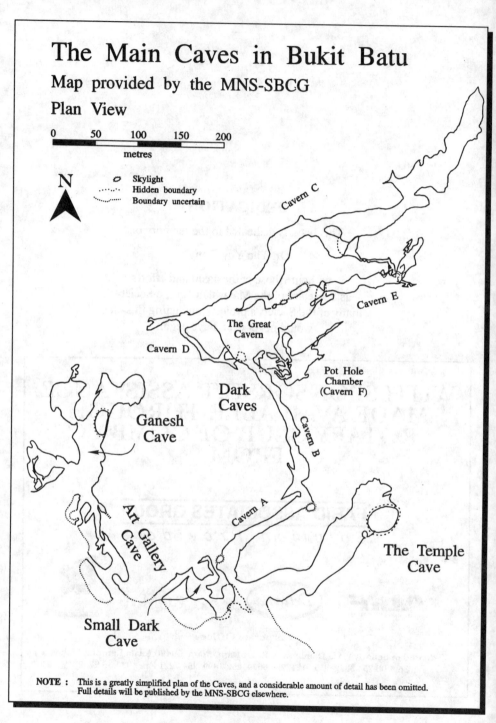

Plan view of the Main Caves at Batu Caves

Acknowledgements

Many thanks to the Malaysian Nature Society for giving me the opportunity, and sponsorship, to write this book.

Many thanks also to all those people who provided me with valuable assistance and information, with special thanks to Ms. Lee Su Win, Dr. P. R. Wycherley, Mr. G. Gopallakrishna, and the MNS-SBCG, and the writers and editors of the 1971 booklet on the Batu Caves.

Last, and most of all,
I would like to thank Charlotte and my parents
for their love, support, and encouragement.

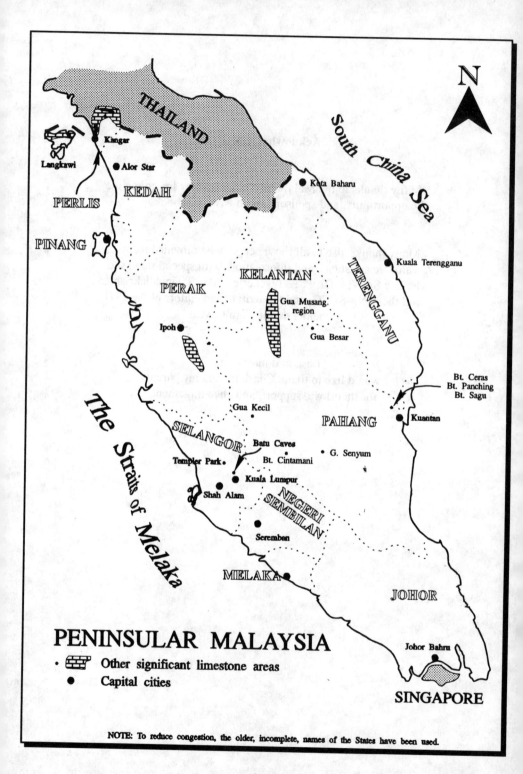

PREFACE

During the 1980's and 1990's, the increasing interest in ecology, conservation, and responsible tourism, has made it imperative that visitors to natural history attractions are provided with better and more relevant information about their conservational status and natural history. The major caves found in Bukit Batu, collectively known as the Batu Caves, near Kuala Lumpur are one such site.

In 1971 a booklet was written about the Batu Caves which did contain a considerable amount of information, but it was written primarily as a tool to assist in the 10 year old campaign to stop the quarrying of Bukit Batu. Happily, although it took yet another 10 years, the fight was eventually successful, and naturalists and tourists alike are still able to visit the Batu Caves to pursue their respective interests. The booklet, having served its purpose, was allowed to go out of print and is no longer generally available.

This new book is intended to provide more up-to-date information regarding the natural history and conservation status of the hill and its caves. It is also hoped that, through this book, at least some readers will be encouraged to take up the sport of caving and may even be inspired to take that extra step and become speleologists.

The emphasis herein is on the invertebrate fauna and ecology of the Dark Caves because it is these features that make the caves worthwhile conserving. Information and photos about the tourism aspects of the Batu Caves are widely available elsewhere, including in the Temple Cave itself.

While this book concentrates on the the Dark Caves, a short guide to the Temple Cave and other Hindu caves is also provided in the section on the Temple Caves. This provides visitors with some immediately useful information about the formations and shrines they see while touring the Temple Caves.

To assist the reader a glossary has been included containing most of the main speleological, technical, and biological terms. An extensive bibliography has also been included, most of which pertains to the Batu Caves, but which also includes references to other Malaysian caves and speleology in general.

A large proportion of information in this book is drawn from the 1971 booklet, and credit and thanks go to all those who were involved in it.

TABLE OF CONTENTS

TABLE OF CONTENTS ix
INTRODUCTION 1
LOCATION... 2
   A short description of Bukit Batu 2
   A short description of the Dark Caves 2
HISTORY... 3
   Archaeology 4
CONSERVATIONAL HISTORY AND STATUS........................... 5
   Specific conservation notes... 7
SCIENTIFIC RESEARCH HISTORY 9
GEOLOGY AND FORMATION OF THE CAVES 10
   Limestone and Cave formation 10
   The Formations 13
THE ECOLOGIES OF LIMESTONE AND CAVES 18
   Limestone Ecology 18
      Limestone Flora 19
      Limestone Fauna 20
   Cave Ecology 20
      Cave Fauna 23
         Cave Adaptations... 23
         Vertebrates 25
         Invertebrates... 28
THE TEMPLE CAVES 32
   The History of Hinduism in Malaysia 33
   The Hindu Religion 33
   The Temples 34
      The Ganesha Temple 34
      The Sri Subramania Swamy Temple 34
      The Vali Devayanai Temple 35
   The Small Dark Cave 35
   The Art Gallery Cave 35
   The Ramayana Cave.. 35
   Thaipusam 36
APPENDIX I — Glossary... 40
APPENDIX II — Other Known Caves In Bukit Batu.................. 44
APPENDIX III — Bibliography And Additional Reading List.... 48

INTRODUCTION

Bukit Batu, and its caves, is the southernmost significant limestone in Peninsular Malaysia, and is by far the Peninsula's best known limestone hill, perhaps even in the whole country. Its proximity to Kuala Lumpur makes it a prime site for tourism. It is renowned for the Tamil Hindu festival of Thaipusam, held at the beginning of every year, where hundreds of thousands of people, both devotees and onlookers, swarm through the Temple Cave over a period of two days.

The Dark Caves, located immediately adjacent to the Temple Cave and generally unknown except to scientists and cavers, consist of approximately 2 km of passages on several levels. They were at one time developed for tourism but, after their closure in 1980, the fittings had been left to decay. The Malayan Nature Society Selangor Branch Cave Group (MNS-SBCG) removed these in the late 1980's, and built a new and better walkway cover in the area where guano dropping from the ceiling was a major problem. In mid-1980's the MNS-SBCG also began taking groups of interested people into the caves by appointment. The main attractions of these caves are their size and formations, and their ecology.

There are, or have been, at least another 16 caves in the hill. Some are developed, some not, some were only discovered in the 1980's, and some have already been lost due to quarrying. Most of these are discussed in various places in this book.

In order to be technically correct, it has been necessary to use expressions in this book which may seem daunting to some readers. To assist those who might have difficulty with such terms, Appendix I provides a glossary which explains the meaning of most speleological (caving) and biological expressions used.

For those who are interested in finding out more about caves and cave ecology, in particular about the Batu Caves, Appendix III contains an extensive bibliography, and the MNS-SBCG can be contacted through the address given on page ii at the beginning of this book containing the publisher's details.

A short guide through the main tourist caves i.e. the Temple Cave, the Art Gallery Cave (previously known as the Museum Cave), and the Small Dark Cave is provided in the section on the Temple Caves.

LOCATION

Bukit Batu is located about 12 km north of Kuala Lumpur, Peninsular Malaysia, just off the main highway to Ipoh. On a global scale, it is located approximately on latitude 3° 14.4' N (i.e. north of the Equator), and longitude 101° 41.2' E (i.e. east of Greenwich). Most taxis will be happy to take a passenger to the Caves, tour buses operate from most larger hotels, and public transport buses also stop there.

The main caves i.e. the **Dark Caves**, the **Temple Cave**, the **Art Gallery Cave**, and the **Small Dark Cave**, are located on the south side of the hill, with 272 concrete steps leading up to the entrance of the Temple Cave. About three quarters of the way up, the path to the Dark Caves leads off to the left.

The entrance to the path leading to the Art Gallery Cave and the Small Dark Cave is at ground level, about 50m before reaching the steps, on the left hand side. The Temple authorities charge a nominal entry fee. The path to these caves is via a zig-zag concrete footbridge which overlooks a pond fed by rainwater run-off and subterranean water i.e. water that has filtered through from the top of the hill. The pond is home to a large number of non-native turtles which have been introduced to the area.

A short description of Bukit Batu

The name means *Stone Hill* in Malay, but it is derived from the name of a nearby stream called Sungai Batu. The stream, described by the caves' European discoverers as "a bubbling crystal streamlet over many-coloured quartz and blue limestone pebbles" is now more of a sluggish, smelly, rubbish- and silt-filled drain.

Bukit Batu consists of the typical tropical limestone hill, steep sided and towering, with dense forest covering most of the top and its natural slopes. Its rugged surface is heavily criss-crossed by deep chasms and gorges formed by the rains of aeons, which dissolved away large portions and formed the 18 or more known caves that exist or existed in the hill.

A short description of the Dark Caves

Of the 18 or so known caves in the hill, the Dark and Temple Caves are the largest and best known. The Temple Cave is described in a section of its own later on in the book. The Dark Caves consist of about 2 km of surveyed passages, some large enough for airplanes, and others so tight that one can hardly crawl through them. They consist of seven major sections named Cavern A through to Cavern F and the Great Cavern (See map of the caves). This highly unimaginative naming system was originally devised in the 1920's by the leaders of the first major scientific research group and, for the sake of convenience, it is still retained today.

HISTORY

The Batu Caves were first discovered by Europeans in July 1878 when a hunting party led by Captain H. C. Syers, Selangor's first Superintendent of Police, caught wind of the aroma of guano wafting through the trees. In this group was an American called William T. Hornaday who was later to record the visit as part of his experiences in Southeast Asia. They visited three caves and collected bats in two of them. It is Hornaday's account that gives the date of the first European discovery of the caves.

The following year Captain Syers led another group to the caves. Included in this group was Mr. D. D. Daly, Selangor's first Superintendent of Public Works, whose account of the discovery and exploration was to be the first, and therefore better known, of the two. It is Daly's paper that is usually referred to when it is stated that the caves were first discovered in 1879; in fact they were only first **reported** in that year. There is, however, also some evidence that indicates that Chinese farmers had begun small scale guano excavation as early as the 1860's.

At the time it was quite an adventure getting to Bukit Batu. The starting point was Kelang, which was then the hub of activity in Selangor. After a two hour steamer ride inland followed by 27.5 km on horseback, 6.5 km of which were through the forest, the explorers arrived at "Kwala Lumpor". Another 14.5 km of jungle track brought them to the foot of Bukit Batu. Neither Daly's nor Hornaday's accounts indicated that they visited the Dark Caves. Of the three caves they both described, only the one they called Gua Lambong (Hanging or Swinging Cave) bears any resemblance to any of the caves known today: in fact it was probably the Temple Cave.

Hornaday even predicted the inevitability of tourism in the next century, describing a natural alcove in Gua Lambong which might shelter a stall selling "refreshments, photographs, and torches". By contrast, Daly described the same niche as a perfect cooking alcove for "the most fastidious Eastern cook".

By 1889 the Dark Caves had been discovered, though by whom has not been recorded, with Mr. H.N. Ridley making the first major scientific explorations of the caves that year, which included the, today inconceivable, conservational sin of dynamiting the floor of the entrance in search of fossils! His work there continued off and on until 1920.

The Temple was founded in 1891 and Thaipusam has been celebrated there since 1892. In the few decades that followed, nothing of much significance to the caves occurred until most of the hill was zoned as a recreational area. In the 1940's the stone staircase was built up to the Temple Cave making it easier for devotees and tourists to reach the Temple Cave and the Dark Caves.

Archaeology

Archaeologically, the caves in Bukit Batu have been among the poorest in Malaysia. Some bits of pottery were found, probably in the cave that is now known as the Art Gallery Cave, and Ridley, through his "excavations" of the Dark Caves entrance, also found some bits of Chinese pottery. He also found a large quantity of bat bones in the floor at the entrance, which he believed came from bats that had died and fallen from directly above. Bats prefer to roost in the dark, which is usually some distance from

> **Did the Temple Cave ceiling collapse shortly after it was discovered?**
>
> There are interesting differences between the observations made by the first three individuals describing what appears to have been the Temple cave. While all three were clearly very impressed with the dimensions of, and formations in, the cave, their descriptions of the end of the cave show definite changes (dates are time of observation, not time of recording):
>
> - **1878** – Hornaday described the entrance of Gua Lambong as a "yawning black hole", and as having a 100 ft high dome at the end of a passage that was 60 feet high.
> - **1879** – Daly described Gua Lambong as a large black hole, with an opening in the ceiling at the end which produced a "soft light" in the cave.
> - **1889** – Ridley's description of the Cathedral Cave (very obviously today's Temple Cave), suggests a much larger cave than Gua Lambong. He also most specifically mentions "a huge shaft about a thousand feet high" open to the sky.
>
> Are these three descriptions all of the same cave i.e. the Temple Cave? If so, it would seem that the roof of the Temple Cave collapsed during the eleven years between its "discovery" and Ridley's explorations!
>
> Hornaday and Daly had to make do with resin torches for lighting, which would not have illuminated very much of the cave. Ridley's highly enthusiastic description, on the other hand, could have been due to the vastly improved visibility that would have resulted from the open shaft, providing a view of the cave much as it is today.

the entrance, and human usage of the caves is usually restricted to the lighter, and therefore nearer, regions of the cave entrance. The presence of bat bones at the modern day entrance and the lack of evidence of human usage in the same area led him to conclude that the prehistoric entrance to the Dark Caves must have been some distance further south and that it, and its ceiling, had fallen away at some time, thereby eradicating any traces of prehistoric human usage of the Dark Caves.

Both Daly and Ridley mentioned some drawings at the entrance of the Temple Cave, which they reported to have been made by the Sakai aborigines. These have long been covered over.

Ridley found monkey bones and evidence of a cooking fire in one of the, now lost, caves that he called the Sakai Cave.

The Besisi aborigines living in the area at the time of Ridley's visit made little use of the ground level caves due to the likelihood of having to compete for possession of the caves with bears and tigers, which were still quite common in those days.

The extensive guano collection from the cave, which began even before the Caves' "discovery", will also have had a thoroughly devastating effect on any archaeological remains that might have been present. The chance of finding any useful artefacts would therefore have quite effectively been eliminated.

CONSERVATIONAL HISTORY AND STATUS

The Batu Caves conservation effort goes back quite a long time, even though the results have not been entirely effective. The conservational status of the fauna and flora of the caves is dealt with in their respective sections.

1860's — The caves were discovered by Chinese farmers, and mined for guano. Previous to this their existence was probably very well known to the aborigines in the area.

1878 — The caves were discovered by Europeans, and their existence subsequently recorded for science.

1920 — A wooden staircase leading to the Temple Cave was built.

1930 — The significance of the caves was recognised by the British Colonial Office, which gazetted most of the hill for Public Recreation.

1939 — One section of the present-day stone and concrete staircase was built. The other two parallel sections were added on later to cater for the increase in the number of visitors.

1954 — The British Colonial Office leased a portion of the hill for limestone quarrying.

1959 — A second quarry lease was issued.

1961 — The Malayan Nature Society (MNS), together with a number of scientists, expressed their concerns and protested against the quarries, but to no avail.

1964 — In order to obtain more public support to stop the quarrying, the Batu Caves Protection Association was formed.

1970 — The Batu Caves were declared a tourist centre. Despite this hopeful sign, one of the leases, which was about to expire, was extended and a third, *government*, quarry was also opened!

1971 — The MNS and the Batu Caves Protection Association jointly produced and published *A Guide To Batu Caves* to assist in the campaign to protect the Batu Caves.

1973 — The Dark Caves were opened to the public. The infrastructure required for this included the, now defunct, funicular railway, the entrance turnstile, the cave lighting, the fake stalagmites at the entrance, and the covered concrete walkways.

1976 — With the publication of the Third Malaysia Plan (TMP) the Malaysian government, for the first time, acknowledged the need for a balance between development and conservation. The TMP recognised the Batu Caves as having unique national heritage value and even proposed them as a national monument. Still the quarrying did not stop!

1980 — Reports of rockfalls in the caves began in April, and became more common as the weeks passed. Other reports stated that the caves were in imminent danger of collapse due to the blasting in the quarries. As a consequence the caves were closed to the public, and it was announced that the quarrying would cease by the middle of June. In July however it was reported that the stoppage had not taken place and that quarrying would be extended for another six months. In September it was further announced that blasting would be restricted to "safe places". The ability of anyone to define "safe places" was however vigorously contested by various, knowledgeable, scientists who had conducted geo-structural analyses of the massif.

1981 — The blasting did finally cease around the time of the December 31st, 1980, deadline, and the MNS published, in the March issue of the Malayan Naturalist, an open letter to the Menteri Besar (Chief Minister) of Selangor thanking him for stopping the blasting at the end of the previous year. An interesting footnote to this is that in 1992, one of the quarry companies was *still* processing limestone, some of which had been blasted from the cliffs before the end of 1980.

1984 — The Malayan Nature Society Selangor Branch Cave Group (MNS-SBCG) was founded. Their primary intention was to explore and map caves in Peninsular Malaysia, and to promote and encourage cave conservation. The Batu Caves became their main training grounds. Their work also includes leading educational tours for schools and other interested groups into the Dark Caves.

1985 — The MNS-SBCG began discussions and negotiations with the Selangor State Government with the aim of taking over the management of the Dark Caves. Since their closure, the Caves had only been visited by groups led by the MNS-SBCG, foolhardy adventurers, graffiti artists, scientists with permits, and local people, who prize the cave cockroaches as fishing bait!

1989 — The Selangor State Government provided the MNS with a grant to clean up the Dark Caves and the immediate surroundings. This enormous task, conducted by the MNS-SBCG, involved replacing the collapsing railings and awnings over the walkways in caverns A and B, and removing almost a century's worth of visitors' rubbish and graffiti, the mock stalagmites and dilapidated hut at the cave mouth, and the power cables and useless, rusty lights that had been installed to light the passages and formations during the caves' tourism heyday. Consequently, a visit to the Dark Caves became a far more pleasant, and natural, experience.

1991 — The Malayan Nature Society submitted a comprehensive management plan for the Batu Caves to the Selangor State Government.

1992 — The Selangor State Government agreed, in principle, to the management of the Dark Caves by the MNS, but the details had not yet been worked out.

Specific conservation notes

This section presents some notes regarding specific instances where conservation, in and around the hill, has not taken place and for which it is now too late, or where it is urgently needed.

— Ardent conservationists and cavers will undoubtedly deplore the ecological and spelaeological disasters that have been wreaked in and around the caves where the temples and art galleries now reside. It must however **always** be borne in mind that if the temples did not exist, it is quite likely that within a few decades **nothing**, except maybe a housing development, would be on the site where Bukit Batu proudly, if a bit damaged, still stands.

— **Bukit Batu may well be only place left in the world where the primitive trapdoor spider,** *Liphistius batuensis,* **is found, and even there it is highly endangered.**

The only other known location was Anak Bukit Takun, a limestone hill a few kilometres further north in Templer Park. It was reported to be present in the hundreds everywhere in Gua Anak Bukit Takun in 1961, but in the mid 1980's only one was found in a relatively inaccessible chamber high up in the cave. The decline in the Gua Anak Bukit Takun population can be directly associated with the loss of the protecting forest surrounding Anak Bukit Takun and the frequent flooding of the cave by the tin mines that were dug directly in front of the entrance to the cave. These mines were excised from the the Templer Park reserve after 1964.

A 1931 study in the Batu Caves reported numbers similar to those recorded for Gua Anak Bukit Takun in 1961. While still reasonably common in the Dark Caves, the population is definitely not as large as previously described. **The general trend appears to be towards extinction.** More information about *Liphistius* can be found in the section on invertebrates.

— In 1961, the cave cockroach (*Pycnoscelus striatus*) was very common throughout the Dark Caves, and was even found at the end of Cavern C. It was most common in the guano at end of Cavern A, where it was found in the thousands. In 1965, no mention of the common house cockroach (*Periplaneta americana*) was made in the, then comprehensive, list of invertebrates. The 1971 guide booklet mentions that *P. americana* occurs in small numbers. By 1984 the *P. americana* population density was of the same order as that of the cave roach in 1961, while the cave roach itself had become a relatively uncommon sight. This suggests that a major ecological upset took place after 1965. The approximate time of change can be further pinpointed by a paper published in 1974, which indicated that the house roach populations had increased after the installation of the lights and the covered walkway in 1973. The cave cockroach is also popular as fishbait and people sneak in to the cave to collect it for that purpose. It seems that, once again, human interference might be at fault. The author of the 1974 paper also naïvely wondered whether the presence of the house roach would have an effect on the cave roach. We now know!

— The only Malaysian collection of the primitive plant *Ranalisma rostrata*, also known as *Echinodorus ridleyi*, was found by Ridley in a location that has been lost to quarrying. The genus is considered to be extremely ancient and is thought to represent a stage in the transition between monocotyledonous and dicotyledonous plants. It has also been found in Indo-China, and other species in the genus are found in West Africa.

— The short-stemmed fan palm *Maxburretia rupicola* is found only on Selangor limestone and nowhere else in the world. Its closest relative is found on the limestone of Langkawi, several hundred kilometres to the north.

— Several caves, originally recorded by Daly and Ridley, can no longer be found. They were most probably lost to quarrying.

— Any archaeological evidence that may have been present in any of the caves, would have been initially disturbed by the guano miners who started work as early as the 1860's. The development of the Dark Caves, the Temple Cave, and associated caves will have completely destroyed the last possibilities of any archaeological artefacts being found.

— Two serow were reported shot in the Batu Caves area in 1989, and no evidence of serow has been found since. The size of the Bukit Batu population is not known, and it is therefore possible that any remaining animals may have moved into the more inaccessible (to humans) interior of the hill's forest.

SCIENTIFIC RESEARCH HISTORY

The Batu Caves are probably the most thoroughly researched caves in Peninsular Malaysia, and it is appropriate that a list of the major research conducted in the caves be presented. The list is by no means complete, and is only intended to provide an overview. It does not include any of the work conducted on individual animal species or genera, such as the work done on the cave cockroach or the white planarian. References to other research done can be found in Appendix III.

1878 — Syers and Hornaday collected some bats from several of the caves.

1889 — H.N. Ridley made extensive collections both in and around the hill. Unfortunately, upon arrival at the British Museum, a couple of boxes of specimens were opened and combined, so that the cave and the forest collections were all mixed up. His first visit to the caves was made by bullock cart and his last visit, in 1920, was made by car.

It is known that the Italian naturalist Odoardo Beccari made collections here around this time too, though they were not mentioned in his book about his work in Borneo.

1913 — Annandale, Brown, and Gravely studied some of the invertebrates in the Dark Caves. The cave cricket was named after Gravely.

1928 — Extensive studies of the cave fauna were conducted in the Batu Caves by a group of scientists led by Cedric Dover and Mercia Heynes-Wood. This was the first attempt to scientifically describe the invertebrate ecology of a tropical cave. Dover devised the system, which is still in use today, of calling the major passages Caverns A-F.

1930 — Bristowe conducted studies on the arachnids (spiders and their relatives) of the Dark Caves. He made some additional observations in 1961.

1959 — McClure conducted a broad range of ecological studies in the Dark Caves for about two years, developing a model of the food network that operates within the Dark Caves, and making numerous other useful observations about population dynamics of several species of animals.

No major research has been conducted since McClure's work, though various students and researchers from all over the world have used the caves for smaller projects. Unfortunately the results for many of these have not been published. The collective knowledge to date is extensive, though far from comprehensive, and an enormous wealth of ecological and other scientific information has yet to be gleaned from the Batu Caves. Many a doctoral thesis is waiting to be researched and written on the ecology of virtually any of the invertebrates found in the Batu Caves, especially the troglobitic ones. The section on Cave Fauna provides a bit more information about these animals.

GEOLOGY AND FORMATION OF THE CAVES

Caves are found in lava, sandstone, ice, and limestone. **Lava caves** (or tubes) are formed when lava flows down the side of a volcano. The outside of the lava flow, which cools faster than the inside, hardens and remains in place. The lava on the inside, which is warmer and therefore more fluid, continues moving at the front of the flow, leaving behind a tube of cooled and hardened lava. While some of these are known to be over ten kilometres long, with various branches and even different levels, they never change in shape, size, or length after their initial formation, nor do they develop new passages as time goes by. Only by collapse of the tube through erosion or some brute force, such as an earthquake or another eruption, can they change.

Sandstone caves form in sandstone cliffs that are, or were at some time, near the sea or a river. The abrasive action of wind, water, and sand, etches passages and even small caverns in the sandstone in a process known as **corrasion**. Usually not very long nor very large, this type of cave usually collapses well before reaching any significant size.

Ice caves are found in glaciers, and are formed when meltwater cuts its way downhill through the heart of a glacier. These caves vary in size and shape, but are very transient, since they may have collapsed, melted away, or frozen up by the next year.

The majority of caves, and the most interesting, are **limestone caves**. They come in all shapes and sizes. Many of them are still changing in shape and size mostly due to the slow, but interesting, process known as **solution** or **corrosion,** with corrasion playing a small part. (See also the inset - The Chemical Basis...)

Limestone and Cave formation

Limestone is formed in the sea, where billions of tiny animals, called coral polyps, extract minerals (mostly calcium salts) from sea water to make a protective surrounding for themselves. This results in huge expanses of coral reef growing in a warm, shallow, sea which, if left undisturbed, can thrive for many millions of years. During this time the calcareous skeletons of the coral and other animals are deposited on top of each other on the ocean floor, together with other particles suspended in the water, as a lime mud in a process called sedimentation.

In the case of Bukit Batu, this occurred during the Silurian period (See Fig. 4. page 14, for details about the ages of the earth), when the whole area that is now Peninsular Malaysia was under the sea. A range of coral reefs must have existed reaching from the north of Malaysia, and maybe further, to what is now Kuala Lumpur, with a couple of isolated spots in Johor and Singapore. During the Triassic period (maybe beginning even earlier, during the Devonian/Carboniferous period), the landmass now known as Peninsular Malaysia was lifted above sea level by the movement of the continental plates in a process known as orogeny, or mountain building. This included all the limestone areas such as Kuala Lumpur, Ipoh, Perlis, Kedah, and Taman Negara. During this process, the limestone was heated, compressed, and folded strongly, metamorphosing it into various forms, including marble, of which most of Bukit Batu consists. By the end of the Triassic period, the central mountain range had been formed, together with large limestone plains, which are also known as karst plains.

As the aeons passed, these limestone plains were subjected to great quantities of rain (see inset) which dissolved the more soluble portions of the limestone plains while eroding the surrounding land, leaving behind the magnificent limestone massifs which today tower above parts of the Malaysian alluvial plains.

The size and shape of the Batu Caves indicates that they were in all likelihood formed before the karst towers came into being, which would place their formation at between 60 to 120 million years ago. Rainwater would have entered the limestone through cracks, faults, and bedding planes from the beginning, to dissolve the limestone from the inside (See Fig. 5, page 16) and forming cave passages. As more and more of the surrounding limestone was dissolved away, these passages became exposed to the outside world, resulting in the caves as we know them. Due to their proximity to each other, it is quite conceivable that the Batu Caves and the Temple Cave were both part of a much larger cave system which collapsed many tens of millions of years ago. The process of cave formation however still continues in many caves, including parts of the Batu Caves.

> **The chemical basis for limestone erosion**
>
> Limestone is essentially calcium carbonate ($CaCO_3$), which dissolves very easily in acid. One very common acid in nature is carbonic acid (H_2CO_3), which forms when atmospheric carbon dioxide (CO_2) combines with ordinary rainwater (H_2O). This is by no means a very strong acid, but when a lot of it flows over and through the limestone for long enough, it will slowly, but surely, dissolve away the limestone.

It should also be noted that not all the caves in Bukit Batu are the same age, nor are all parts of a single cave necessarily the same age either. Caves generally form at the water table level. Thus the vertical position of a cave in a hill can be used to provide an indication of the cave's age, since the water table would have started at the top and moved its way down i.e. the higher the cave, the older it is.

> **Some Cave Records**
>
> While portions of the Dark Caves are large in cross-section and length when compared globally, it's dimensions are nowhere near record values. The following are some examples of world records.
>
> The deepest cave known to date is found in France and is called the Reseau Jean Bernard. Its lowest point is 1602 m below its highest entrance. By contrast, the deepest point known so far in the Dark Caves (the potholes in Cavern F) is about 130 m below the highest entrance (the skylight in the Great Chamber) and about 50 m below the normal entrance level. (which makes it about the same level as the bottom of the staircase leading up to the cave.)
>
> The cavern with the largest volume is the Sarawak Chamber, which makes up the lion's share of Lubang Nasib Bagus (Good Luck Cave) in Mulu National Park in Sarawak, Malaysia. It's volume is estimated to be on the order of 12–13 million m^3 compared to the next largest, Deer Cave, also in Mulu National Park, the volume of which is estimated to be around 5 million m^3. A rough estimate of the volume of **ALL** the known caves in Bukit Batu, passages and caverns included, gives them a **total** volume of less than 2 million m^3.
>
> The longest and most extensive cave system in the world is the Mammoth Cave/Flint Ridge system in Kentucky, USA, with a total length of about 560 km, spread over more than half a dozen inter-connected levels. The Clear Water Cave system in Mulu was extended in 1990 to make it the 7th longest in the world at just over 100 km. By contrast, the Dark Caves are on the order of 2–3 km long.

The oldest known cave in Bukit Batu is therefore Gua Pandan. As the water table sank, Cavern E was formed, followed by the Temple Cave, the main sections of the Dark Caves, and the Upper Ganesh. The most recent caves include are the Art Gallery Cave, the Small Dark Cave, Ici Bawah, and Lower Ganesh, and of course the lower parts of Cavern F. However, since the water table is now about 100 m lower than the known caves in Bukit Batu, it is highly likely that numerous other caves exist in the limestone below ground level, but which are either covered by or filled with alluvial soil or mud.

Most caves in Malaysia are thought to have initially developed phreatically, as described above, progressing on to vadose development as the passages got larger and larger. The Batu Caves are no exception. Passages with smooth, rounded, ceilings were formed phreatically, and this is typical of most passages in the Dark Caves. Only the passages at the bottom of the pothole in Cavern F (The Pothole Chamber) are predominantly vadose, and these are still in the process of developing. As the passages get wider, either phreatically or vadosely, the ceiling's structural strength is no longer sufficient to support it and sections of the ceiling begin to fall away until it once again becomes structurally stable. If stability cannot be achieved, then the ceiling collapses completely, as it did in the Great Cavern in the Dark Caves, in the Temple Cave, or anywhere else where there is a hole in the roof. The Great Cavern is a good example. The floor is littered with huge chunks of rock which have fallen from the ceiling, and there is a wide, open skylight where the roof collapsed completely. Some of the limestone blocks, weighing several hundreds of tonnes, are the size of small houses.

Photographs of the shaft in the Temple Cave during the 1960's, before it was cleared and concreted, show the rubble at the bottom, which must have been the result of the ceiling's collapse.

There are indications that the Batu Caves experienced at least two, if not more, major episodes of vadose development i.e. the river rose and ran at least twice through the Caves for long periods of time. The surfaces of some of the stalagmites in the Caverns C and D have been worn smooth and the finer details on the stalagmites have been blurred. This suggests that the passage was formed when the river ran through the first time, after which the stalagmites formed. The second time the river ran through, it started re-dissolving the stalagmites but then dried up again before it could complete the task. Other stalagmites nearby, which must have developed after the river receded for the second time, have fine, sharp, and clear details on their surfaces. The period between the growth of the smoothed stalagmites and the return of the river is not known, but judging from the size of the stalagmites, it could have been between several thousands of years to quite possibly hundreds of thousands of years!

The Formations

The most obvious things one notices upon entering a cave are the formations. In a film, play, or photograph, the distinctive silhouettes of stalactites immediately tell the viewer that the scene is taking place in a cave.

Stalactites are the very quintessence of caves, and it is in order to see them that many people enter caves, sometimes risking life and limb, and at times ignoring most of the other, less obvious, attractions the cave might offer. Their often unearthly beauty, or their resemblance to recognisable figures, has led to the creation of numerous legends concerning their origins in certain caves. The combination of the resulting tourism, worship, and general ignorance have also been instrumental in the ecological deaths of many caves.

Stalactites are not the only type of formation; a large number of other cave formations exist, and they are known by a variety of names depending on their form and position. Thus, apart from stalactites or stalagmites (both are called "stal" by cavers), one can find curtains, flow-stone, rimstone, straws, rafts, pearls, gour pools, columns, dripstone, fans, corals, shields, bubbles, and a number of other things. The technical term covering them all is **speleothem**.

The basic component of all these formations is calcium carbonate [$CaCO_3$]. The most common form is known as limestone (*batu kapur* in Malay). In another form it is known as marble. A third form is calcite, and that is the one of most interest here. Though chemically no different from limestone or marble, calcite does have a different crystalline structure, which leads to the production of many interesting formations.

Era	Period	Epoch	(Millions of Years Ago) Began
CENOZOIC "Age of Mammals"	Quaternary	Recent	—
		Pleistocene	2
		Pliocene	6
	Teritary	Miocene	25
		Oligocene	38
		Eocene	53
		Paleocene	65
MESOZOIC "Age of Reptiles"	Cretaceous		136
	Jurassic		190
	Triassic		225
PALEOZOIC "Age of Amphibians" "Age of Fishes" "Age of Invertebrates"	Permian		280
	Pennsylvanian		320
	Mississippian		345
	Devonian		400
	Silurian		440
	Ordovician		500
	Cambrian		570

Fig. 4. The ages of the Earth

Calcite develops when limestone is dissolved by naturally acidic rain water to form chemically unstable calcium bicarbonate [$Ca(HCO_3)_2$] according to the following formula:

$$\underset{\text{Limestone}}{CaCO_3} + \underset{\text{Carbonic acid}}{2H^+ + CO_3^{2-}} \Rightarrow \underset{\text{Calcium bicarbonate}}{Ca^{2+} + 2HCO_3^-} \Rightarrow \underset{\text{Calcite}}{CaCO_3} + H_2O + CO_2$$

This solution makes its way down to the water table, percolating through the cracks and faults in the limestone bedding planes. The limestone re-crystallises as calcite when the calcium bicarbonate-saturated water emerges from the cracks into the air of a cave passage or cliff overhang, and releases water and carbon dioxide according to the above formula.

Depending on the chemical impurities it may have accumulated on the way down, the colour of calcite may range from pure white to solid black. It can even be transparent, depending on how it has crystallised. The most common colour in Malaysia is a rusty red-brown resulting from iron compounds found in the soil.

The entire process, which results in the final, colossal, formations we sometimes see, can take between thousands and millions of years. Even small formations of less than a centimetre in length can take decades to form. Irresponsible cave visitors (usually humans) tend to forget, or ignore, that fact and take great pleasure in breaking off bits and pieces, sometimes very large ones, as a test of their own strength or as souvenirs. The large pieces generally prove too heavy to carry and are usually left where they fall, and small, delicate ones are often dropped not far from where they were taken because they have already broken into little pieces. Daly himself in 1879 admitted to having collected samples of the formations!

Some formations and crystals are not made of calcite, but these are normally quite small and less common, though by no means less attractive. They consist of a wide range of minerals which occur in small pockets in the limestone.

Though the process of speleothem development is a slow and tedious one, it does result in some of the most beautiful, fascinating, and even astonishing, creations of nature.

The best known of these are stalactites, stalagmites, and columns, all of which are related to each other. The **STALACTITE**, which hangs from the Ceiling, often begins as a small cave straw (see below) which gets larger and wider as more calcite saturated water flows over and through it, constantly depositing thin layers of calcite over the previous ones, thus building it up.

Very little is known about the growth rate of Malaysian stalactites. What is known is that stalagmites (see below) in other tropical areas grow at a maximum rate of about 2 mm in thickness a year, with an average growth rate of tenths of a millimetre per year. This suggests that a stalactite or stalagmite with a diameter of about 10 cm (a size that is easily broken off and taken away by uncaring and selfish souvenir hunters) could take, on average, about 500 years to grow!

STALAGMITES, which are on the Ground, are usually found below stalactites. As the water drips off the stalactite, it splashes onto the ground where more calcite can crystallise. Because the impact spreads the water over a larger area, stalagmites are usually wider than the stalactite overhead. Exceptions abound however, due to differing water flow-rates and micro-climatic conditions present in different caves. Thus one may find enormous stalagmites with little or no stalactite above them, *vice versa*, or tall thin stalagmites, or short squat ones. If situated in a passage through which a gentle but steady breeze passes, both stalactite and stalagmite may be at an angle downwind away from the vertical!

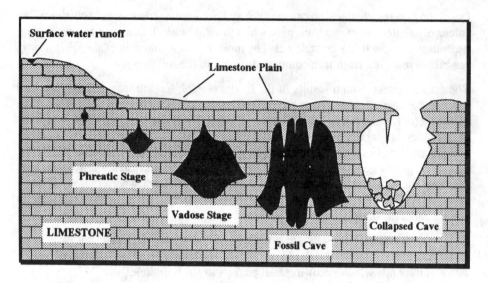

Fig. 5. A simplified version of the stages of cave formation and collapse.

When a stalactite and a stalagmite have grown to such an extent that they meet, the result is a **COLUMN**. These can range in size from a few tenths of a metre in height and a few centimetres in diameter to enormous structures several tens of metres high and several metres thick! A magnificent column can be found about two thirds of the way into Cavern C, and a large one can be found on the left hand side at the top of the steps at the end of the Temple Cave.

GOUR POOLS or **RIMSTONE DAMS** are formed when the saturated water deposits calcite at the edge of a pool which has resulted from slow flow of water. The deposit on the edge builds up over the years, until it forms a basin. Usually, a series of basins is formed giving rise to very attractive cascades. Gour pools vary in size from that of a thimble to that of a small swimming pool! The Geometric Pool in Cavern D is an attractive, but not very large, example of a gour pool.

CAVE STRAWS are incredibly delicate structures and are usually no more and no less wide than a drop of water! Occurring where water drips through slowly in very small amounts, they begin by crystallising minimally around the edge of a drop of water hanging from the ceiling. The next drop adds a bit of crystal to the previous deposition, and this continues until a straw is formed. In temperate climates, straws can reach a length of a couple of metres, but in Malaysia they generally don't exceed 25cm, and then only in relatively undisturbed caves. This is predominantly due to differences in the climatic and atmospheric conditions. Another probable contributing factor to their lack of length in public or easily accessible caves is that most casual cave visitors have a tendency to test the strength of the straws and take a bit home. Longer straws may well exist in some of the more inaccessible caves, such as those found in Mulu National Park in Sarawak. A few small ones can be found in the deeper recesses of Cavern D.

Short straws can sometimes be seen hanging from the ceiling of concrete parking garages and from the bottoms of bridges only a few months after they were constructed. While the end result is essentially the same as those found in caves (cement is made from limestone), the process by which they are formed is chemically different because of the processing that the limestone has undergone to make cement.

FLOW-STONE is a very apt term for the formations which arise when water is not able to drip freely from floor to ceiling but instead runs down the cave wall, depositing the calcite over a wide area; the result being that flowstone can look like a petrified waterfall. A magnificent example of this can be seen in Cavern B.

CURTAINS, DRAPERIES, or **SHAWLS** are formed when the water runs along the same narrow path on an inclined ceiling, depositing calcite along a winding trail. The resulting formation can have folds and falls like a real curtain, but not as flexible. Some of the more spectacular ones are translucent, and might even be banded with several colours due to periodic impurities. Shawls can reach a length of several metres.

CAVE PEARLS form in very much the same way that real pearls do, except without the help of an oyster i.e. the calcite grows in layers around a nucleus. The similarity even extends to the fact that oyster-made pearls are also made from $CaCO_3$, but with yet another different crystalline structure. The technical term for those more than 2mm in diameter is *pisolites* (from the Greek words meaning "pea-stones").

HELICTITES are peculiar, yet very attractive, formations that look a bit like solid cave-straws which twist, turn, and spiral out from any surface in the cave, quite oblivious to the pull of gravity. Ranging in thickness from about one millimetre to almost one centimetre, their colours can vary from translucent white to solid black. These are probably the most mystifying of formations. It is still not quite certain how they are formed, but it is thought that their unusual shape is due to the unevenness with which calcite saturated water is forced out of the very small tube that exists down the centre of the helictite, and the subsequent way that crystallisation takes place.

CAVE FLOWERS are an exception in that they are made of $CaSO_4$ (calcium sulphate) and not $CaCO_3$. This form of $CaSO_4$ is known as gypsum, and the formations are consequently also known as **GYPSUM FLOWERS**. Easily recognisable, they are translucent white, and are twisted and turned like butter scrapings, or like toothpaste squeezed from its tube. One of the differences between cave-flowers and helictites is that the former grow from the base, while the latter grow at the tip.

There are many other extremely attractive crystal formations, made of either calcite or another mineral. Some of these form on the cave surfaces through seepage, some form through deposition, some form in small pockets, while others cover the surfaces of entire chambers. In both the latter cases, the crystals probably formed entirely under water, and it is only a question of volume which makes it a pocket or a chamber. The chambers however tend to be largely calcite crystals, while the smaller ones may consist of other minerals.

THE ECOLOGIES OF LIMESTONE AND CAVES

Limestone hills support two very distinct ecologies; one is on the surface, and the other is in the caves below. Bukit Batu and its caves are of particular ecological interest for a number of reasons. As mentioned earlier, Bukit Batu is the most thoroughly researched limestone hill in Peninsular Malaysia, mostly because of of its proximity to Kuala Lumpur and several of the main Malaysian universities. Both Odoardo Beccari and Henry Nicholas Ridley, two of the "fathers" of Malaysian natural history, conducted studies and made collections in and around Bukit Batu over 100 years ago. Ridley, having been commissioned by a Committee of the British Association for the Advancement of Science to "collect their living and extinct fauna", spent considerable effort on the caves and even went to the extent of blasting the compacted guano and mud floor of the Dark Caves' entrance in search of fossils and indications of human habitation! (Neither was found). The concept of conservation in those days was obviously somewhat less well defined compared to now, though the practice these days is often not much better! Dover's group in 1929 attempted for the first time to scientifically describe the invertebrate ecology of a tropical cave.

Limestone Ecology

The most distinctive feature about Malaysian limestone ecology is its plants. Many species of plants will grow only on limestone, and because of the relative isolation of karst towers, many species of plants are endemic i.e. are found only on a particular hill or hills. Plants and animals that live on and around limestone hills are a severely threatened group. The threats to which they are exposed include destruction of habitat due to quarrying, repeated fire-clearing of the surrounding land for agriculture, and clearing of land for development, such as temples, especially those that use ground level caves. Good examples of the latter are the many temple caves around Ipoh in the State of Perak. In the case of burning, the original plants are replaced by pioneer plants such as *lallang* grass (*Imperata cylindrica*), bamboo, *Macaranga* spp., and an introduced species of small tree (*Piper* sp.) related to pepper which is found all around Bukit Batu. Under normal circumstances these would usually be succeeded after a few years by the original plant species. Repeated burning or clearing however does not give the original ecology the time to re-establish itself and the pioneers grow again each time.

Bukit Batu is home to a number of endemic plants and probably quite a few smaller endemic vertebrates, such as frogs, and invertebrates, such as snails.

Limestone Flora

Plants growing on limestone make up an important part of the Malaysian flora. While limestone covers only about 0.3% of the surface of Peninsular Malaysia, it is home to around 14% of the Peninsula's plants. Of these, almost a third are endemic to Peninsular Malaysia, and a sixth are confined to limestone.

Another factor which increases limestone plants' risk of extinction is that a good proportion of them, including orchids, gesneriads, begonias, and balsams, are of considerable horticultural interest.

Many orchids are ideally adapted to the harsh and infertile environment offered by limestone, and many epiphytic species, such as *Coelogyne*, *Bulbophyllum*, and *Eria* spp. can often be seen flourishing on the side of a limestone cliff where most other plants cannot even get a foothold. The terrestrial orchid, *Calanthe vestita*, was originally recorded in Malaysia only from Bukit Takun and Bukit Batu. Elsewhere, in Thailand and Burma, it is also found away from limestone. Some species of the highly prized slipper orchids, (*Paphiopedilum* spp.) also prefer limestone habitats. One species, *P. niveum*, which is endemic to the Langkawi islands, is in extreme danger of extinction in the wild due to overcollecting. It is however very common in orchid fanciers' greenhouses!

Among the more interesting gesneriads (commonly referred to as the African Violet family) is the aptly named *Monophyllaea* genus, so named because the plant usually consists of just a thick succulent stalk with a single large leaf at the end. Another genus, *Paraboea*, is conspicuous by its silver-grey leaf-rosettes contrasting with the dark of the high, almost sheer, cliff faces on which it lives. The colour is a result of the severe dehydration that takes place at the high temperatures that can occur on these cliff faces. They somehow manage to survive the dehydration and re-absorb water the next time it rains to come up looking lush and green again! *Chirita* species, yet another gesneriad, are conspicuous by their attractive, large, and usually blue flowers.

Begonia phoeniogramma is a very pretty, small plant whose dark green leaves often have fine white spots. It is quite common in undisturbed, moist areas around the lower scree slopes of Bukit Batu, and occasional specimens can be seen growing between the rocks on either side of the steps leading up to the Caves. It was originally recorded there by Ridley and, several years after his first visit, he expressed some concern about the survival of this plant due to the disturbance that both the devout and tourists were causing. The construction of the steps helped in the conservation of this plant in this part of the hill.

Maxburettia rupicola is an attractive, short-stemmed, fan palm that is only found on Selangor limestone. *Pandanus calcicola* is a large pandan (also known as screw-pine because of the way the leaves grow in a spiral) found in the dense forests on top of the hill. Several specimens can be seen on the cliffs on either side of the steps.

Limestone Fauna

At the end of the last century, Ridley reported that tiger, pig, bear, deer, elephant, *serau*, and hornbill were all found on and around the hill. Today, with the hill entirely surrounded by residential and industrial development, it is highly unlikely that any large animal except the *serau* can still be found on Bukit Batu, and even this may be in danger of local extinction.

The serow, or *kambing gurun*, is a shaggy, donkey sized, goat that is the Malaysian equivalent of a mountain goat and is ideally suited to the limestone surface terrain where it is most commonly found. Signs of its presence are often found on limestone ledges. It does not, like most other animals, leave its droppings wherever it happens to be at the time. Instead, it has regular "toilet" spots. These are marked by conspicuous heaps of pea-sized pellets, in various stages of drying out due to their relative ages, ranging from the oldest, white, ones through various shades of brown, to the freshest ones which are almost black. See also **Specific Conservation Notes**.

Since a snail's shell is essentially made of $CaCO_3$, limestone hills are probably the best place a snail could choose to live, from the point of view of availability of building material. As in the case of some plants, there are numerous instances where snails are found on one limestone hill only and nowhere else. Bukit Batu has several such species.

Dusky leaf monkeys (*Presbytis obscurus*) were seen from the cave steps in the 1960's though none have been recorded recently. Banded leaf monkeys (*P. melalophus*) have also been seen recently on the cliffs on the right hand side of the steps. The long tailed macaque (*Macaca fascicularis*) is very common around the caves, and can be seen frolicking in the branches of the trees high up in the shaft at the end of the Temple Cave, and begging for food in the the cave, along the steps, and at their base.

While not much is known about frog and toad ecology on limestone, it has been suggested by at least one biologist that, due to the surface topography of limestone hills, the best way to collect limestone frogs is to look in the caves! Frogs and toads living on the surface sometimes fall through skylights, and can afterwards be found hiding under rocks and in nooks and crannies below.

Cave Ecology

The ecology of caves is a most intriguing one. It exists in the almost total absence of sunlight and yet, as any visitor to the Dark Caves will attest, it can support extremely high density populations of animals, often higher than those of similar animals on the outside (but with much the same species diversity)! Sunlight is the primary source of energy for almost everything alive today, but for obvious reasons very little of this can be found in caves. In order for a sunlight based ecosystem to exist in caves, there must be some means of transporting the energy inside. Here bats and swiftlets play a very important role. They bring energy into caves in the form of their guano or droppings. By the time this takes place, the sunlight has already gone through a couple of processing stages, as illustrated in the energy flow chart in Fig. 6.

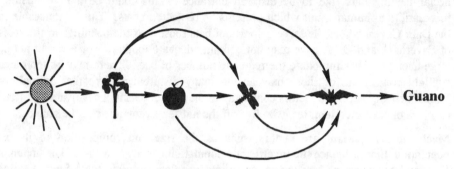

Fig. 6. Energy flow into cave ecosystems

The food chain/energy flow within the cave is more complicated and is not provided here, though it can be found in McClure's publications. Although guano is a waste product, it is also appears to be the result of a wasteful metabolism, because the guano of fruit bats still contains sufficient nutrition to support very large populations of invertebrates. However, since the main source of energy in a cave is guano, this means that a cave ecosystem is a relatively closed one and therefore very sensitive to small changes, especially with respect to its restricted energy source. Hence, a disturbance to the bats means a potentially disastrous disturbance to the rest of the cave's inhabitants.

Not all caves support a diverse ecology, and there are several reasons for this. One of the main reasons is people. If the existence of a cave has been known to humans for some time, then it is very likely that they have used it for some reason or other. Most often they make fires for light, warmth, cooking, or to keep insects away; sometimes they make fires for no reason at all. Lighting fires seems to fulfil primaeval urges in some people. The smoke from these fires bothers the main vertebrates, the bats or swiftlets, which then abandon the cave. The swiftlets also suffer further indignities from birds' nest collectors. As a consequence, the invertebrates' primary source of food, guano, is not renewed and they die out. If people aren't busy making fires, then they need guano to fertilise their plants. The guano mining in the Batu Caves intensified very soon after its discovery, and the cave floors are scarred with pits, many over 2 metres deep, where the guano has been dug up. Along the sides of Caverns A and C in particular, a darker section beginning at the present-day floor level delineates the pre-guano mining floor level. Until recently, these pits were full of rubbish left behind by the thousands of tourists who visited the cave in the past! Guano mining leaves the invertebrates without food since the guano cannot be replaced as fast as it is removed. It may take several decades, if not centuries, to deposit a one metre thick layer of guano on a cave floor!

To be fair however, bats can also be very fussy. A cave may not have the right conditions in which they like to roost. Because they do not possess sonar, fruit and nectar feeding bats like to be near an entrance. This could be a high opening inaccessible to humans, but which presents no obstacle to bats. This is noticeable in the Dark Caves, where the large colonies of bats roost near the openings in the roofs of Caverns A and C. A cave may not contain adequate footholds, or it might not be large enough to accommodate the requisite number of bats. There may be too much sunlight coming in, or there may be too many disturbances by other animals or human beings. All these factors contribute to the lack of bats in a cave, and this leads to a lack of cave invertebrates, who live off the nutrients remaining in the guano.

Much more important are factors, such as the size and composition of its bat population, that influence the invertebrate population density in a cave. The guano of fruit- and nectar-eating bats is very nutritious when compared to that of insect-eating bats, whose predominantly chitinous droppings would hardly be considered good fare by any animal. Thus if the bat population contains fruit eaters, there is a greater likelihood that there will be a large number of invertebrates in that cave. Another contributing factor is the density of bats in a cave, and the area covered at that density. Two or three bats per square metre are hardly enough, but are 20, or would 200 be sufficient to support a large population of invertebrates? A look at the ceiling of some of the heavily populated caves suggests that it may be closer to the latter figure!

Consequently, only about one in ten caves in Peninsular Malaysia supports a significant animal population. Among these are the Dark Caves at Batu Caves, Gua Lipas in Gunung Panas (Raub), Gua Cintamanis in the hill of the same name (near Karak), Gua Daun Menari and Gua Anak Daun Menari in Batu Luas (Taman Negara).

Notably, all of the above caves manage to retain their invertebrate populations because they are protected from humans in some way or other. This may be because of physical obstacles such as in the case of Gua Cintamanis, which requires a tiring scramble up a steep slope, and then down a 12 metre cliff, inside the cave, using special climbing equipment, or in the case of Gua Daun Menari, which is at least an hour's walk from Kuala Kenyam in Taman Negara, which is some distance from Park headquarters. Gunung Panas is in what was a security area, and visitors needed a police permit, and the Dark Caves have a locked gate to prevent people from going in on their own and getting lost.

Cave Fauna

In caves, as anywhere else, there are basically two types of animal life – invertebrates and vertebrates. By far the best known cave animals are the bats, but caves are home to literally hundreds of other animal species. The Batu Caves support over 200 different species of animals, most of which are invertebrates that depend heavily on the presence of guano provided by the bats roosting in the caves.

They can all be roughly classified into three categories according to the amount of time they spend in the caves.

1. **Trogloxenes** (cave visitors). These only use the caves for temporary shelter e.g. from the rain or sun. Some, such as the frogs mentioned earlier, may also be accidental trogloxenes, i.e. they did not intentionally enter the cave. Humans are trogloxenes, as are bats and swiftlets.

2. **Troglophiles** (those who like caves). These may spend their entire life cycle in caves, but could survive just as easily outside. Caves just happen to provide the right conditions for them, such as darkness and dampness e.g. the Cave Centipede, *Scutigera decipiens*.

3. **Troglobites** (those who live in caves). Such animals live their entire life cycles in caves. This does not necessarily mean that they are not found on the outside. Troglophiles such *Scutigera* can therefore also be called **facultative** troglobites i.e. they can choose to be troglobitic and conduct their whole life cycle in the caves. On the other hand, **obligate** troglobites, such as the trapdoor spider *Liphistius batuensis* or the Cave Cricket *Diestrammena gravelyi*, are usually never found outside caves. In some case, such as *Liphistius*, they are only ever found in one specific cave or group of caves.

Cave Adaptations

Why is such a fuss made over obligate troglobitic (cave adapted) animals? The following section might shed some light on the reasons for this excitement.

The ancestors of most troglobites would typically have been troglophiles to begin with, and therefore most likely pre-adapted. Good modern examples would include the cave centipede (*Scutigera decipiens*) and the tailless whip scorpion (*Sarax brachydactylus*). Their pre-adaptations include long legs and feelers, and a liking for dark, moist nooks and crannies.

In the very remote past, the cave populations, for various reasons, became separated from the outside populations, but somehow managed to survive. After thousands of years, and tens of thousands of generations, either or both populations evolved to the point where they became species distinct from each other. The existence of a troglobitic species is therefore a relative indication of how long a cave has supported a flourishing ecology.

If a species, such as *Liphistius batuensis,* is restricted to a limited range of limestone hills, it might be because the hills were at one time connected to each other, thereby allowing the animals to become more widely distributed. This was most likely the case with the Selangor limestone hills, where *L. batuensis* is found. In that situation, one possible conclusion is that the species evolved before the hills were formed. Troglobitic animals are therefore **sometimes** an indicator of prehistoric connections between limestone hills. A close parallel situation occurs on the surface with the fan palm *Maxburettia rupicola.*

Such conclusions must however be made with great caution, and corroboration should be sought elsewhere, such as in the geological record. An example of where such a conclusion would be incorrect can be found in Sarawak, where the hairy and flightless earwig *Arixenia esau* is found in both the Niah Caves and the Mulu Caves, which are a considerable distance apart from each other. As it turns out, this earwig is a parasitic symbiont of the Naked Bat (*Cheiromeles torquatus*), which is found in both caves. The more likely conclusion here is that bats transported the earwig from one cave to the other, since the caves and their hills were probably never physically connected.

Some troglobitic species have lost their pigmentation and are white (sometimes translucently so) in colour. This is known as albinism. They have often also lost the use of their eyes, which may even have disappeared. This can be attributed to a combination of energy requirements and natural mutations. When a natural mutation appears in an animal, it is not usually sufficient for the mutation to be simply harmless. In order for a mutation to survive, it should provide its owner an advantage over unmutated animals.

In the forest, an albino animal, for example, would be very conspicuous and would quickly fall prey to enemies. In a cave, it cannot be seen and so can survive. However, the fact that its albinism is not noticable is not sufficient for a new species to evolve since, in the darkness of a cave, lack of colour by itself provides no significant advantage over the coloured individuals. However, characteristics such as albinism, sightlessness, and eyelessness also require less energy expenditure since pigment, vision, and eyes are not required and therefore need not be produced and maintained. Since energy is at a premium in a caves, the resulting energy savings provide a distinct, long term, passive advantage over "normal" competitors. In the case of active advantages, such as overdeveloped limbs or feelers, e.g in the cave cricket, *Diestrammena gravelyi*, the extra expenditure of energy is compensated for with the improved chances of survival from predators.

Animals that appear white are found in the Dark Caves. Not all of the these however are **obligate troglobitic**, and some are discussed further on.

Vertebrates

Most vertebrates found in caves are troglophilic and some, such as the cave racer (*Elaphe taeniura*), are possibly facultatively troglobitic, with comparatively few being obligate troglobites. None of the vertebrates found in the Batu Caves so far are in the latter category. Except for humans, the usual trogloxenes e.g. bears, leopards, porcupines, and wild pigs, have not been recorded in and around Batu Caves recently for reasons mentioned earlier.

Best known of all cave vertebrates are the **bats**. Estimates of the Dark Caves population run as high as a quarter of a million animals, comprising at least nine species, with the most common being the frugivorous Dog Faced or Cave Bat (*Eonycteris spelaea*) and the Diadem Horseshoe Bat (*Hipposideros diadema vicarius*). Horseshoe bats are insectivorous, and their collective name is derived from the shape of the skin folds around their mouth, which are used to direct their ultrasonic signals that they use for echo-location. The Diadem Horseshoe Bat is also named for the white, diamond-shaped patches on its shoulders.

Bats constitute the **largest** group of mammals in Malaysia, maybe even in the world, and they play as important a role in non-cave ecology as they do in caves. Unfortunately they are not known well enough by most people, and are therefore much maligned. Here are some facts about bats:

- Insectivorous bats consume numerous tonnes of flying insects each night, many of which are either harmful to humans e.g. mosquitoes, or crop pests.

- Nectivorous bats i.e. those that eat nectar, are instrumental in pollinating a number of tree species. Most notable among the plants they pollinate are various *durian* species (*Durio* spp) and several mangrove species. While many people could probably live quite happily without the former, the latter are far more essential to human well-being. Mangrove swamps help prevent the silting up of river channels and estuaries by trapping mud and debris, allowing clear channels to form, and thereby aiding in the prevention of flooding after heavy rains. The trapping of mud and silt also eventually leads to the creation of new land. In addition, mangroves are very important as breeding grounds for prawns, crabs, and many commercial species of fish. The bats from Batu Caves range as far as Port Kelang or further to feed on (and therefore pollinate) the mangrove flowers.

- Not all bats use sonar. Frugivorous bats rely on their eyesight and sense of smell to find food and to find their way around. This is why they roost within sight of cave entrances. Insectivorous bats however do use sonar to detect food and their surroundings, and will therefore quite readily roost in the darker parts of caves. It has also been established that, in order to sort out their own individual signals and species signals, bats have long been using modulation techniques that are almost identical to those used in modern electronic sonar and radar technology!

- Bats memorise their way around a cave because the ultrasonic din from the thousands of roosting bats echo-locating would sound to them much like the stock exchange during peak trading hours sounds to us. That is why bats in a cave sometimes fly into one's face. A person walking down a passage is an unexpected obstruction and gets noticed only at the last moment. People behave the same way for some things e.g. when going to the bathroom at night many people don't bother to turn on the lights because they know the way. We've all experienced what happens if the furniture along the way has been moved without our knowledge!

- Frugivorous bats are very important in dispersing of seeds of the fruit they have eaten. Seeds with hard, indigestible, coats can pass through the bats' digestive systems unharmed and, since not all the guano is deposited in caves, they may be spread far and wide. The seeds of some species MUST actually pass through an animal's digestive system in order to germinate, because the digestive juices soften the hard seed coat.

- Vampire bats do exist, but are not found in Malaysia. They are native to South America. They also do not suck blood using hollow teeth like straws! They use their teeth to scrape the skin, which their prey doesn't always notice because their saliva has some anaesthetic properties, and then they **LAP** up the blood.

- Ironically, it is the much maligned and persecuted members of the harmless, attractive, frugivorous, flying-fox species found in Malaysia whose name is *Pteropus vampyrus*. It is in this group that the largest bats, and some of the most endangered species in the world, are found, some with wingspans of over a metre. Their common name derives from their appearance, which resembles that of a dog or a fox. Recent research also suggested that, on the basis of physiological and neurological characteristics, flying foxes might be descended from primates, unlike the smaller bats which are descended from rodents. This was subsequently refuted on the basis of DNA analyses and other methods. Flying foxes roost in trees and do not usually shelter in caves.

- Orchard owners claim that frugivorous bats affect the fruit harvest by damaging fruit. While this may be true in some instances, by and large, bats generally go only for the already ripe fruit which is too far gone for successful harvesting and marketing. They thereby actually help in the prevention of fruit flies which are not as selective about the fruit ripeness!

Several species of **swiftlets** and **swallows** also nest in caves, and they perform very much the same role as the insectivorous bats when it comes to providing guano. Some species nest in the dark portions of caves, such as Lubang Nasib Bagus in Mulu, and even employ a simple form of echo-locating for navigating in the dark, while others prefer to nest in the brighter areas. However, where there is a large population, such as in the Niah Caves in Sarawak and Tiger Cave in Thailand, they are usually severely disturbed due to the human penchant for their saliva in the form of their nests! Fortunately, swiftlets never seem to have shown much interest in the Batu Caves, and so the Caves were spared the ravages and indignities inflicted by bird's nest collectors.

The **Blue Whistling Thrush** (*Myophonus caeruleus*), which is quite common around Malaysian limestone, has been found flying back and forth in the Pot Hole Chamber of the Dark Caves without colliding with the walls, but with an erratic flight path and chattering incessantly. This behaviour suggests that this species also uses a primitive form of echo-location. This bird is responsible for the little heaps of crushed snail shells found on ledges around limestone hills. In remote areas, the shells are only from snails found on and around the particular hill, but near urban areas, the shells of *Achatina fulica*, the introduced, but now widespread, Giant African Snail, are also found mixed with the limestone snail shells.

Several species of **snakes**, including a 2m long python, have been recorded in the Dark Caves, but only one species is regularly encountered. The **Cave Racer** *(Elaphe taeniura)* is a troglophile, since it is also found on the outside, but there is some evidence to suggest that there may be a troglobitic population in the caves. While this species normally has stripes along the entire length of its body, the cave variety's stripes are limited to its tail. Its pale colour originally caused it to be

> **Some things never change!**
>
> Ridley collected a number of of specimens of the the cave racer (*Elaphe taeniura*), and shipped them to the British Museum. They were lost during transport when the shippers misplaced them while trying to cut their costs.
>
> Ridley had insured the shipment but was unable to obtain the full insured amount despite considerable correspondence with the insurance company. It was suggested to him that they might discuss it if he would care to visit their home offices in England!

misclassified as an obligate troglobite by Ridley, who collected several specimens last century. McClure kept several specimens captive for more than a year and through several moults, and their colour did not change to match specimens found on the outside, which suggests the existence of a troglobitic population. So far, however, no solid evidence, such as very young snakes, has been found to confirm the existence of the troglobitic population. Reaching a length of up to 2 metres, the Cave Racer is a back-fanged snake, therefore nominally venomous, though not dangerously so to most humans. Captured ones will try to bite their captors with the sides of their mouth in order to use the venomous fangs. This snake has the ability to crawl up cave walls which, to humans, appear to be almost perfectly smooth. Once having reached the roof of a passage, the snake might do one of two things: if it has reached a bat roost, it will try to grab a bat, and if no bats are there it will hang with its head down, mouth wide open, literally waiting for a bat to fly into it! Bearing in mind that bats fly mostly by memory while in the dark portions of caves, the chances of success are reasonably good. Once a bat has been caught, the snake, despite being venomous, constricts its prey before swallowing it. The prey is poisoned while already on the way down the snake's gullet.

The **toads** *Bufo asper* and *B. melanostictus* are classic examples of troglophiles. These are the same species as those found in Malaysian gardens hiding under rocks and in empty flower pots. Specimens have been found in the caves, particularly in Caverns A and B, that were several times larger than those found in the garden. Ridley measured one 9 inches (22.5 cm) long, and had had reports of larger ones. This is probably due to the steady and good source of food available. They were reported to have become less common since the Dark Caves were developed for tourism, when the entrance was blocked by gates and walls. This, combined with the fact that most specimens were found in Caverns A and B suggests that the toads entered the cave from the front, rather than via the ceiling holes like the frogs mentioned earlier. This is another instance where the development of the cave interfered with its ecology.

Rats and shrews have also been recorded in the Caves. The former are probably accidental trogloxenes and the latter appear to be both troglophilic and troglobitic.

Invertebrates

Though the vertebrates, such as the bats, are immediately noticeable, closer inspection of the walls and the floors can reveal a fascinating abundance of invertebrates whose numbers and variety seem never ending. Only a few of the more interesting ones are presented here; the majority of them will be left out since it would require a volume or two to discuss them all.

Most of the invertebrates in the Dark Caves tend to fall within the last two categories given at the beginning of the section on fauna. The troglobites are usually not found outside caves; indeed, some species are found only in a particular cave and nowhere else in the world.

The largest group of invertebrates found in caves is the insects. The next largest group is the arachnids which include spiders, scorpions, ticks, and mites. Though not as numerous, the myriapods (consisting basically of centipedes and millipedes) are very conspicuous. Other groups including snails, flatworms, and isopods are present but are not as commonly encountered.

Though these groups are well represented both inside and outside caves, the population density of invertebrates found inside is considerably higher. Large numbers of invertebrates are found especially in caves with large bat or swift populations, because the vertebrates produce guano which, being on the bottom of the invertebrate food chain, is the basis for the whole invertebrate ecosystem in caves.

In the Dark Caves alone, well over 200 species of invertebrates covering seven Orders have been listed, including snails, worms, moths, and mosquitoes. The list is by no means complete, since new species are being discovered continually. The most extensive list to date was published by McClure in 1965 with about 150 species. It was not long before more were discovered, including over 50 species of mite, many of which were new to science, and determined researchers should not find it difficult to discover at least one unrecorded species, often also new to science, on any given visit. If you have ever been to a cave with a similarly thriving invertebrate population, and have seen the area that that must be covered by the scientists, then you will appreciate why all the animals have not already been found.

There are many natural factors that dictate the presence of invertebrates in caves which have not been disturbed by humans. These include the micro-climatic conditions within the cave e.g. light, temperature, and humidity.

Another factor which protects the invertebrate population in a cave is that facet of human nature called squeamishness. The parts of caves which support life tend to be muddy, full of guano, smelly, and absolutely seething with these invertebrates, and most people are unable to find enthusiasm for such conditions.

Seething is a very appropriate word! In some places in the Dark Caves one can see more cockroach than wall, and in other places a casual scrape on a thick dry guano bed reveals dozens of animals crawling through it. After a heavy rainfall, guano gets wet from water dripping from the ceiling, and all the animals living in the guano come to the surface and cover all the rocks and walls, e.g cockroach instars (sub-adults), millipedes, and beetles to name but a few. The guano literally heaves and flows like a thick liquid with a life of its own! Within half an hour of being disturbed, the guano surface can be smooth again, having flowed back into place due to the constant activity of the the animals below.

It is possible to observe invertebrate behaviour much more closely and easily in caves than would be possible outside.

Scutigera decipiens, the cave centipede, is a beautiful brown and white striped centipede up to 8 cm long with long legs and feelers, and with the ability to inflict a nasty, poisonous bite. Its head also looks like it should be the tail. Since *Scutigera* is also found in the forest, this may be a camouflage characteristic. Its mating behaviour can sometimes be observed where the male passes a packet of sperm to the female, which she then inserts inside herself to fertilise her eggs.

The cave cockroach, *Pycnoscelus striatus*, distinguished by the bright markings on its thorax and the stripes on the abdomens of the instars has, in 1992, been almost completely supplanted by the plainer, hardier, and more aggressive, common house cockroach (*Periplaneta americana*) in the Dark Caves as well as in other caves around the country. Though *Periplaneta* is being parasitised by a species of wasp, this does not seem to be making an impact on their numbers. The section on **Specific Conservation Notes** details the progression of the species changeover.

Both species can be observed during their moulting stages, with the vulnerable white instar waiting to dry and harden into the familiar brown colour. *Pycnoscelus* is ovoviviparous, meaning that its eggs hatch while they are inside the female, whereas *Periplaneta* lays an egg case containing a number of eggs. These eggs are commonly encountered in the household when cleaning hard-to-reach places.

These and many other things are extremely difficult to see outside caves because they often take place under fallen leaves, inside rotten tree trunks, or in small holes. The animals' behaviour is observable in caves because both the troglophiles and the troglobites consider themselves comparatively safe in the darkness and go about their everyday business in the open rather than hiding away in some small nook or cranny.

The nest of the primitive spider *Liphistius batuensis* can be seen on walls and in nooks and crannies with 6-10 thin silk lines extending radially from one end. These act as triplines, and the spider, which hides behind the trapdoor with a foot between the junction of each pair of lines, can sense when prey crosses the lines. When the prey has come close enough, the spider flips up the trapdoor, darts out, grabs the hapless prey, and drags it back in again, all in the wink of an eye. But, if the hunted turns out to be a hunter instead, (such as a cave centipede) the spider has a contingency plan! It snaps the door shut, rushes to the other end of its tube-shaped silk and debris nest, opens a similar (but without triplines) emergency exit trapdoor, and runs out to hide somewhere.

> **The World's Rarest Spider**
>
> The Trapdoor Spider, *Liphistius batuensis* is an invertebrate of note. It is found only in and on Selangor limestone hills and the fact that there are only three limestone hills in Selangor would tend to make *L. batuensis* reasonably uncommon. Indeed, this genus has been listed as the rarest spider genus in the world by the Guiness Book of World Records. There are only fourteen species of *Liphistius* in the world, nine of which were only described as late as 1984, and eight of the fourteen are found in Malaysia.
>
> *Liphistius* spiders are often referred to as living fossils because of their resemblance to fossilised spiders of the Carboniferous period (about 300,000,000 years ago!).
>
> What makes them obviously different from other spiders is that their abdomen is partially segmented, like that of a wasp for example, when other spiders all have smooth abdomens.
>
> *L. batuensis* may be on the verge of extinction if nothing is done soon to protect them. (See also **Specific Conservation Notes**)

It was first recorded in 1929, but might have been recorded almost thirty years earlier from Ridley's collections if not for a mix up at the British Museum with a couple of his collection boxes, where specimens from the caves were inadvertently mixed with specimens from the nearby forests!

It is worthwhile noticing some of the changes that some of the invertebrates have undergone in the process of adapting to darkness, be it the darkness of a cave or of a rotten tree trunk. One of the obvious changes is the elongation of their appendages in comparison to their bodies. This adaptation gives them a distinct advantage over their short-legged cousins, by enabling them to detect their enemies from further away. Particularly noticeable are the legs and feelers of the Tailless Whip Scorpion (*Sarax brachydactylus*), Cave Cricket (*Diestrammena gravelyi*), and the *Scutigera* centipede. In many cases the legs and feelers are several times longer than their bodies!

The Cave Cricket, like the *Scutigera* centipede, has brown and white markings, and has exceedingly long feelers. Its body may be only 2 cm long but the feelers may be as long as 6 cm.

The Tailless Whip Scorpion is a flat, wide, brownish black animal whose body can be 5-8cm long, but has a "feeler span" of up to 35cm! Its eggs hatch while inside the mother's egg pouch, and the young are carried on her back until they are large enough to fend for themselves. This is the same as with real scorpions, representatives of which are also found in caves.

At certain times of the year, the seasonal misfit stream (see Glossary) flowing through the guano in Cavern C can be found teeming with the white planarian or flatworm, *Dugesia batuensis*, which was long thought to be endemic to the Batu Caves. A coloured specimen was however recently was found in a forest stream. Nevertheless, it is most common in the Dark Caves, not only in Cavern C but also in other seasonal puddles in Caverns A and B. When the puddles dry up, they burrow into the guano and encyst themselves until conditions become more favourable.

Included among the other invertebrates found in the Dark Caves are the 5 cm long, grey, *Glyphiulius* millipede, a scavenger that is found in great profusion on decaying bat carcasses. Ticks and mites that prey on bats are present and case moths, whose larvae make camouflage cases out of indigestible bits of guano are common in the dryer guano. There are assassin bugs (*Bagauda* spp.) which use their preying mantis-like claws to attack small invertebrates and suck out their juices, crickets that live with ants, an endemic crustacean *Parabathynella malayana*, which lives in seasonal puddles, a millipede (*Doratodesmus* sp.) that resembles a section of a backbone and which might be an obligate troglobite, very light coloured snails (*Opeas* spp.) that don't react to light, and which might also therefore be obligate troglobites, a transparent, wormlike, fungus-gnat larva that suspends many sticky silken threads from the ceiling to trap flying invertebrates, the orange and black Mole Cricket (*Gryllotalpa fulvipes*), and long-legged huntsman spiders which don't spin webs, preferring to roam around looking for prey. Even a fireflies can be found in the Dark Caves, though these are probably accidental trogloxenes.

These are but a few examples of invertebrates found in the Batu Caves. There are many more, equally interesting and well deserving of study, and all add to the fascination of caves. Together, with the guano on which they feed, they constitute the bottom section of the food chain in a very fragile ecosytem which is rapidly being destroyed by humanity's need for limestone as a base material for building roads and houses.

There is now a desperate need in Malaysia for a master plan on limestone conservation, wherein certain limestone areas and their surroundings should be set aside as nature reserves for scientific study and/or recreation areas, which will be inviolate forever! The remaining areas can then be exploited for industrial and commercial purposes while still preserving limestone flora and fauna in the protected areas; thus satisfying both the conservational and the commercial requirements.

THE TEMPLE CAVES

A number of the caves in Bukit Batu have been adopted as temples by the local Hindu population. Only the largest however is known as the **The Temple Cave**. This was probably the cave called Gua Lambong by Hornaday and Daly, and Cathedral Cave by Ridley. In 1891, not long after the cave's discovery, Mr. K. Thambusamy Pillay, the founder President of the Sri Maha Mariamman Temple in Kuala Lumpur, established the Sri Subramania Swamy Temple inside the cave.

Hindu priests are now permanently in residence, and considerable redecoration and reconstruction of the cave, and several other nearby ones, has taken place through the addition of colourful statues of the various Hindu deities associated with the cave. The cave floor has been concreted over everywhere and steps built where rubble slopes used to be. At the foot of the steps there are now also Temple management offices, food and souvenir shops, and a school for local children is also situated on the premises.

The Temple has had so much influence locally that most of the development in the area is due to its existence. It is also largely due to the Temple that the caves still exist, since its religious significance and its tourism value contributed greatly to the cessation of nearby quarrying in very late 1980.

The cave is located at the top of an arduous climb of 272 steps which are divided into groups of 17. Today all devotees and tourists alike must climb these in order to see the cave in its full glory, though in the mid-1970's one could ride a funicular railway, for a fee, as far as the entrance to the Dark Caves. Daunting as this climb may seem, it must be relatively easy compared to the effort which would have been required before the 1920's, when no steps had yet been built. The easier, but less fulfilling and less attractive, alternative is to buy a postcard at the bottom of the steps showing the cave lit with coloured lights. In fact, photos of the Dark Caves during their tourist days can still be bought, when they too were lit with coloured lights. The lighting for the temple was first installed in 1952 and then improved in 1967. The labour and funds were provided voluntarily by Hindu staff of the National Electricity Board.

It is not difficult to appreciate why the cave was chosen for a temple. Ridley's name for it, Cathedral Cave, recognised its appropriateness. Its gothic arches and vaulting columns and flowstones would awe even the most irreverent visitor. It is not long, but it is huge! The cave, essentially just an enormous passage up to 50 m wide and 70 m high in places, ends after only a couple of hundred metres in a huge, round, funnel-like, shaft which opens to the sky, its steep slopes covered with greenery among which troupes of long-tailed macaques can frequently be seen swinging. The bottom of this shaft is now concreted over and level, but photographs from the early 1970's show it to have been a mass of rubble and large boulders which were the legacy of the shaft's creation.

The History of Hinduism in Malaysia

Though the term Hindu was originally derived from the name given to the people who lived along the river Sindhu in India, it now applies to the faith of four fifths of the population of India, the people of Nepal, the people of the Indonesian island of Bali, and scattered populations throughout South-east Asia.

Balinese Hinduism is a relic of the time when Hinduism was the main religion throughout a large section of South-east Asia. The Hindu Kingdom of Sri Vijaya held sway in Peninsular Malaysia for approximately 600 years, ending its reign during the late 13th century A.D. By this time, Arab traders had begun the process of converting the region to Islam, and it was completed by the end of the 15th century, shortly before Malaysia was "discovered" by the Portuguese searching for spices and gold. Many Malay ceremonies and customs still bear traces of Hinduism, and the Malay language contains numerous words which are of Sanskrit origin. One of the most commonly encountered ones is the word *jaya* as in *Petaling Jaya*.

Hinduism did not become a significant religion in the area again until after 1884 when an ordinance was passed by the Federated Malay States, as it was then called, which resulted in large numbers of Indian workers emigrating here in search of work. Most of these were Tamils i.e. from southern India and of Dravidian, rather than Aryan, origin, and most of them practiced Hinduism. It was not long before they outnumbered all other ethnic representatives of the Indian sub-continent in the Malay Peninsula.

The Hindu Religion

Hinduism is the oldest religion in the world, with a history of at least 5000 years. The Hindu belief is that it is even older, with no beginning and or end, for it is also called the *Sanatana Dharma* or Eternal Religion. To scholars, it is the Brahmanical

Faith, since to obtain *Brahman* (the Universal Soul) is the ultimate goal of all sincere believers.

Hinduism, as with all other religions, has had a profound and lasting influence on the many cultures with which it has come into contact. The converse is also exceptionally true for Hinduism, though it is not as pronounced in other religions; it is a gentle faith which does not advocate the eradication of, nor does it seek to subdue, existing beliefs when they are encountered, but absorbs and accommodates them. It is extremely flexible and tolerant, with an eclectic mixture of customs or codes that have been liberally adopted from the various cultures it has encountered. Hinduism does not dictate absolutely the way of worship but allows people to do so according to their own spiritual experiences and abilities.

Thus, while the fundamental Hindu belief is that there is only one God, its flexibility permits people to worhip Him in His numerous aspects, according to their abilities and needs. Consequently, by some accounts, there are over 50,000 different representations of the one God!

The Temples

The history of the discovery of the Temple Cave can be found in the chapter on History, and the general history of the development of the Temple can be found in the section preceding this one.

The Ganesha Temple

At the bottom of the steps, a temple was constructed in 1992 and dedicated to one of the sons of Shiva known as Ganesha (also known as Ganesh or Ganesa, Ganapati, and Vinayaka), the remover of obstacles, who is the first deity to be worshipped during any ritual. He is corpulent and awkward to remind us that external beauty has no bearing on internal beauty and spiritual perfection. He rides a mouse, to show that all beings, great or small, are equal in God's eye. His elephant head symbolises intelligence, the snake around his waist represents cosmic energy, the noose represents worldly attachments, and his hook is to prod humanity on the path to righteousness. His broken tusk is to remind us that it was used to write the *Mahabharata* as dictated by the Sage Vyasa.

The Sri Subramania Swamy Temple

This is the main temple at the Batu Caves, and it is dedicated to the other son of Shiva, the Lord Subramania, known as the Lord Muruga by the Tamils. Subramania is the guardian of the world's spiritual progress, and his main symbol is the *vel* or spear which represents the developed and sharp intellect. He rides a peacock to warn us against pride and egotism.

Appropriately, and probably for historical reasons of logistics, his shrine is the most humble one in the Cave. It is located in a small, natural alcove on the left hand side just before the steps rising into the shaft at the end of the cave. Inside, the dominant feature is a *vel* which is kept decorated with fresh flowers and lit with oil lamps.

Scattered throughout the rest of the cave are six more shrines and displays which represent the six temples, in southern India, in which the Lord Muruga abides. These are at Alagarkovil, Thiruchenthur, Thiruparamkundram, Thiruthanni, Swamimalai, and Paloni. All of them are on hilltops, which made the Temple Cave, with its simple and natural, yet awe inspiring appearance, the obvious location when a site was sought for the Temple in Kuala Lumpur.

The Vali Devayanai Temple

Another temple was also completed in 1992, this time at the the bottom of the shaft at the far end of the cave. Its construction was according to standard practice for the temples; hundreds of volunteers, including tourists, carried the large quantities of sand and stone up the steps and to the end of the Temple Cave. This temple was dedicated to Valli and Devasena, the consorts of the Lord Muruga, who represent Jnana Shakti, the power of knowledge, and Kriya Shakti, the power of action, respectively.

The Small Dark Cave

This is the first of the art gallery caves encountered after traversing the lake on the raised walkway. The concept of art galleries was introduced in 1972 by Mr. N. Veeriah, a former Temple Chairman, and the art gallery caves were completed by 1973. The aim was to give the general public an idea of the breadth and greatness of Hindu art and culture. Thus the statues in this gallery mainly illustrate episodes of the *Mahabaratha* and other Hindu scriptures. Included also are various reincarnations, or 'avatars' of the Lord Maha Vishnu.

The Art Gallery Cave

This is also known as the *Valluvar Kottam*, and is dedicated to the poetic works of the Tamil poet Saint Thiruvalluvar. The unique feature of his poetry is that it is supposed to have overcome all aspects of race, religion, or time, and it applies to one and all. His works, written over two thousand years ago, are said to be everlasting in nature and, having thereby transcended human shortcomings and barriers, have earned an immortal place. This poetry has been translated into several languages.

The Ramayana Cave

Formerly known as the Ganesha cave, it is the latest of the art gallery caves and, at the time of writing, had not yet been fully developed. It is the furthest west of the art gallery caves and has an upper and lower section. The upper section is reached via a climb up a scree slope, but steps will be constructed in the very near future. Both sections will be developed.

When completed it will, through the use of statues and murals, depict the great Hindu epic saga after which it has been renamed.

Thaipusam

Each day, as many as a few hundred worshippers and tourists might climb the steps to offer prayers and take pictures. Nothing however even approaches the spectacle of the Thaipusam festival when several hundred thousand spectators and worshippers throng up the long staircase into the Temple Cave and back down again.

When asking or giving thanks for blessings, good health, wealth, protection from evil, general well-being, peace, happiness, or prosperity, or something more specific, such as having a child, spouse, or some other close family member, including oneself, recover from a terrible illness, passing an exam, getting a certain job, or even for forgiveness for some sin, most people who believe in God will offer a prayer and maybe make a silent vow of some kind. The Tamil Hindus in Malaysia, on the other hand, can be much more explicit when asking, or giving thanks, for the fulfilment of their prayers and desires.

> **The *Pooja***
>
> The simplest form of obeisance a devotee can make is known as *pooja*, where the devotee provides the priest with his or her name, or the name of the person(s), and their birthstar(s), for whom blessings from the deity are sought. The priest then recites appropriate prayers on the seekers' behalf for a period of 5 to 10 minutes, after which the holy camphor flame is presented to the deity to signify the energy of transmission of the prayer.
>
> The flame is then brought down to the devotee(s) who receive the warmth of the flame as a physical sign of the deity's blessing, after which they are given '*prasatham*' in the form of holy ash which is applied to their forehead. A spoonful of milk or holy water is then received with open palms and drunk, and a mixture of sandalwood and vermilion paste is also applied to the forehead.
>
> During Thaipusam, with its hundreds of thousands of devotees, this is obviously not possible. In this case, the priest periodically perfoms mass prayers and pots full of milk are are poured over the '*vel*' to signify the completion of the penance undertaken by the devotee. The milk is usually substituted with coconut milk in the Batu Caves.

On one day a year, called Thaipusam (pronounced *tie'pusem*; "tie" as in "neck**TIE**", the "u" pronounced as in "p**U**sh" and the "e" pronounced as in "giv**E**n"), myriads of devotees of the Lord Murugan go to the Batu Caves Temple to give thanks to him for his help and protection by performing an obeisance.

A few of the hundreds of thousands of people, however, may choose to carry a *kavadi* (pronounced *kah'vedee*, with the emphasis on the first syllable, and the first "e" also pronounced as in "given"). This choice, and the celebration that goes with it, has given rise to one of Malaysia's best known and most spectacular festivals.

For those using the Gregorian calendar the particular day in question falls on a different day each year, somewhere between the middle of January and the middle of February, since it is based on the lunar Tamil Hindu calendar. The name of the festival is derived from the name of the month during which it falls (*Thai*) and the day itself, which is the day of the full moon (*pusam*), the middle of the month for the Tamil Hindus.

On the eve of Thaipusam, the statue of Lord Murugan, which normally resides in the Sri Maha Mariamman Temple in Kuala Lumpur, is suitably decorated and prepared for an outing, and placed on a wood and silver peacock chariot together with statues of his two consorts. The next morning the chariot is drawn by bullocks in grand procession to the Temple Cave, and carried up the steps by the devotees and priests. Around this basic ceremony revolves the rest of the festival of Thaipusam, of which the most notable aspect is the carrying of *kavadis*.

The basic *kavadi* consists of a narrow, wooden, tray somewhat less than a metre long, spanned by a wooden arch decorated with flowers and peacock feathers. It contains one or two bowls of milk, which should not be spilt, and some other offerings such as fruit, more flowers, and rock sugar.

There is however virtually no limit to the complexity of the *kavadi*, which can become so elaborate that some of the more complicated ones are massive, pagoda-like, constructions requiring considerable strength and endurance to carry up the 272 steps. These are usually carried by those giving especially profuse thanks.

While carrying the *kavadi*, the devotees further underline their sincerity by having short skewers piercing their tongues, or long shafts going through one cheek and out the other, or have various fruits or bells hanging from their backs, shoulders, chests, and/or stomachs with the help of hooks through folds of skin!

Women too carry *kavadi*s, usually the smaller ones described above, and they don't often have more than a skewer through the cheeks or tongue, but their dancing tends to be somewhat more frenzied, in part probably because their load is less. Nor is the activity limited to Tamils either; Chinese and Caucasians sometimes also carry *kavadi*s, including the larger ones.

The *kavadi* carriers start preparing as much as a month earlier, with a strict, vegetarian diet, complete chastity, and much fasting and prayer. By the end of that month they are able to put themselves into a trance in which they are almost unaware of anything except that they have to go up those steps. They seem to feel no pain and generally don't bleed from their wounds, both while carrying the *kavadi* and afterwards.

During the early dawn hours of Thaipusam, the *kavadi*-carriers are prepared for their ordeal at a river nearby and, when ready, they slowly make their way along the road to the Temple in what seems like a never ending procession.

The procession goes in a reasonably orderly manner, as one after the other they whirl and dance, the bells on the *kavadi* and their bodies jingling madly. They rarely utter a sound themselves. At times they appear to be dancing to a rhythm of their own, despite the fact that drummers are interspersed throughout the procession, beating out a guiding pattern. The specific beat of the drums may not be as important as the very rhythm itself, which probably acts to enhance the self-hypnotic state into which they have entered. Unable to swallow properly or drink because of the spikes through their tongues or cheeks, the saliva sometimes runs thickly out of their mouths, (though generally it seems to be kept well under control), which together with their sweat-matted hair, gives some of them a somewhat wild appearance.

As they make their way to the steps leading to the cave, they often lose their direction with all their gyrating, and friends and helpers who accompany them must turn them back in the right direction. The helpers sometimes also help by chanting "*vel, vel, vetri vel*" (The Spear, the Spear, the Invincible Spear). As their eyes stare blankly, focusing at some far off point, one cannot help but wonder what they see.

Upon reaching the Temple grounds, they make their way up the steps to the cave itself, sometimes resting a bit at each landing. The steps are divided into three sections. Two narrower ones on either side and a wider one in the middle. The main crowd goes up the left-hand-side section and those carrying a *kavadi* go up the middle. Everyone comes down the right-hand-side.

Inside the cave the *kavadi*-carriers follow a large loop to the end of the cave, where they perform a few last whirls, say a prayer, and then are divested of their kavadi and their skewers. Spikes through the cheeks, or anywhere else, are simply pulled out and the affected area wrapped, if possible, in a red cloth (just in case they do bleed, which isn't often). Otherwise they are just unhooked! After that they walk out of the cave with everyone else, almost as though nothing special had happened!

Normally, large, dense, crowds such as this one can be quite frightening and threatening, and the press of bodies and the smell of sweat and excitement and camphor can to be very overpowering. The Thaipusam crowd however doesn't inspire any such feelings and, on the contrary, it is easy to be caught up in the excitement yourself! There is no animosity in the crowd, no one is specifically trying to push you out of the way, and no one objects if you jostle them a bit in an effort to get somewhere. The crowd literally flows, unstoppable, up the stairs, packed back-to-belly, like an ant colony on the move, and anyone already half-way up who changes his mind about completing the trip has about as much chance of actually doing so as a snake has of wearing shoes.

Down below, on either side of the trail of people going up to the cave, festivities abound in a riot of colour and smells. Stalls peddle spiced Indian sweetmeats of all sorts, religious figurines and writings are sold by the hundreds as are incense sticks and cubes of camphor, and the coconut sellers make a brisk business, even far down the road, where their wares are brought in by the truckload!

Eventually, as dusk approaches, everything dies down and people start drifting off home. It is not easy though if you came by taxi or were given a ride, because everyone is now competing for the taxis which come by. If you came with your own car, chances are that you had to park it as much as a kilometre or more down the road, and had to walk in just as you now have to walk out. The Lord Murugan will not be going home until the next day, when he will slowly make his way back to the temple in town, arriving at night by torchlight after much festivity along the way.

APPENDIX I — Glossary

While this glossary may not be as complete as might be desired by some, it attempts to provide meanings for most of the less commonly known words used in this book.

alluvial	Pertaining to alluvium, which is soil built up by materials such as silt and sand that have been transported by rivers and floods.
arachnid	An animal in the spider family. This includes spiders, ticks, mites, scorpions, pseudo-scorpions, whip-scorpions, tailless whip scorpions, daddy-long-legs, and schizomids. Representatives of all of these can be found in the Dark Caves.
batu	The Malay word for "stone".
bedding planes	The layers in which a sedimentary rock, such as limestone, is laid down. The gaps between these layers represent weaknesses in the integrity of the limestone, through which water can flow to make caves.
bukit	The Malay word for "hill".
calcareous	Made of calcium carbonate [$CaCO_3$].
calcite	When limestone dissolves in very slightly acidic (due to atmospheric carbon dioxide [CO_2]) groundwater, and later crystallises out again the result is calcite. Most cave formations consist of calcite.
caver	A person who responsibly enters and explores caves for his or her enjoyment. See also **speleologist**.
chitin, chitinous	The substance which forms most of the hard parts of insects. From the Greek *chiton* meaning tunic.
corrasion	The process whereby a material is worn away by the physical action of wind, water, or particles.
corrosion	The process whereby a material is worn away by chemical action.
dicotyledonous	Having two cotyledons. The seeds of dicotyledonous plants have two more or less equal halves when germinating. This is one of the two main divisions into which flowering plants are divided. See also **monocotyledonous**.
doline	A pit caused by corrosion, usually with a reasonably large diameter, in the surface of limestone hills and plains. These often lead to caves passages below.
echo-location	See **sonar**.
endemic	Found only in a specific region, the size of which is not particularly defined e.g. endemic to Malaysia, endemic to Batu Caves. This is usually applied to animals or plants.
facultative	The situation where an organism can survive in more than one environment e.g. living in caves or the outside. See also **obligate**.
fauna	The animals of a region or epoch.
flora	The plants of a region or epoch.

frugivorous	A frugivorous animal is one that eats fruit. See also **nectivorous** and **insectivorous**.
gour, ghar, gaur	Also known as rimstone pools and rimstone dams, these are formed in the path of slowly flowing water, where calcite builds up at the downstream edge of a pool in one continuous region, eventually building up into a wall which dams the stream which formed it. Can range in size from 1 cm to several metres in diameter.
gua	The Malay word for "cave"
guano	The droppings of bats and cave swiftlets - from the Spanish *guano* or *huano* meaning dung. Used as fertiliser.
helictite	One of the many **speleothems** found in caves. These are described in the section on formations.
insectivorous	An insectivorous animal is one that that eats insects. See also **frugivorous** and **nectivorous**.
invertebrates	Animals which do not have a vertebral column or backbone.
kambing gurun	See *serau*.
karst	Originally derived from the Slovenian *kar* (rocky) and/or *hrast* (oak), the expression was first used by Austrian mapmakers in 1744 to describe the rocky, oak-forested limestone and cave region in northwestern Yugoslavia and northeastern Italy. The word now is used to refer to any area where the surface topography consists mainly of dissolved rock.
kavadi	A structure carried on the shoulders of Hindu devotees making a petition during ***Thaipusam***.
limestone	The end result of millions of years, generations of coral reefs, and the high temperatures and pressures generated by geological folding of landmasses. The main constituent is calcium carbonate ($CaCO_3$), which comes from the inorganic remains of marine invertebrates, of which corals make up the largest portion.
marble	One of the forms limestone can take when subjected to the high temperatures and pressures which occur during geological movement.
metamorphose	To change shape or quality. A caterpillar metamorphoses into a butterfly.
misfit stream	A (usually) small cave stream which is not the one that originally formed the passage.
monocotyledonous	The seeds of monocotyledonous plants have only one cotyledon. See **dicotyledonous**.
nectivorous	A nectivorous animal is one that eats nectar. See also **frugivorous** and **insectivorous**.
obligate	The situation where an organism **must** live in a certain environment in order to survive. e.g. living in caves. See also **facultative**.
orogeny	Geologically speaking, a mountain building episode. From the Greek *oros* (mountain) and *genesis* (production).

phreatic	A phreatic (pronounced free-attic) cave passage is one in which the walls, floor, and ceiling were formed while still entirely below the water table. Many of these exist, still water and mud filled, deep under Kuala Lumpur. They are often encountered by civil engineers, much to their dismay, who are trying to provide solid foundations for buildings!
pisolites	Cave pearls (see section **History - Formations**)
pooja	The prayer said by the priest on behalf of the devotees who come to the Batu Caves Temple.
scree	The sloping mass of debris, consisting of rocks and earth, found at the base of a cliff. From the old Norse *skritha* for slide.
sedimentation	The process whereby solid and semi-solid materials suspended in water are deposited on the sea bed, gradually building up layers of material. These are compressed by their own weight, and the forces imposed on them during orogeny, to form sedimentary rock such as limestone, sandstone, and shale.
serau	Also known as *kambing gurunn* in Malay, it is the donkey-sized Malaysian equivalent of a mountain goat and has the scientific name of *Capricornis sumatraensis*.
skylight	Any opening in the ceiling of cave that lets in daylight. It is usually a result of the collapse of a portion of the ceiling.
sonar	A detection system, also known as echo-location, used by bats (and some birds) where they bounce ultra-sonic sound waves off objects in their path and listen to the reflections to obtain information about the objects' size and position. This technique is also used by humans in electronic form. It is similar to radar except it uses sound waves instead of electromagnetic waves.
speleologist	A person who conducts scientific studies of caves and their origins. Such a person probably started out as a **caver**.
speleology	The study of caves. From the Greek *spelaion* (cave) and *logos* (*study*).
speleothem	Any natural cave formation. From the Greek *spelaion* (cave) and *thema* (deposit).
stalactite	The classic, conical, cave formation which hangs from the ceiling (Can be remembered by the fact that it has a **C** for ceiling" in it).
stalagmite	The classic, conical, cave formation which rises up from the ground, usually below a stalactite. (Can be remembered by the fact that it has a **G** for ground in it).
supersaturated	The situation when a crystalline solute, such as **calcite**, is dissolved in a solvent, such as water, in such high concentrations that the addition of just a small crystal of the solute will cause most of the dissolved solute to crystallise out of the the solution.
symbiont	An animal or plant that lives in **symbiosis** with another one. One of the partners in a symbiosis.

symbiosis	A situation where two or more organisms of different species live in close association, without harming each other, for mutual benefit. In some cases the individuals will not survive without this association.
Thaipusam	A Tamil Hindu festival (See the section on *Thaipusam* in the main text)
troglobite	An animal that spends it entire life cycle in caves.
troglophile	An animal that can live on the outside, but prefers to live in caves, and may do so for its entire life cycle. It such an instance it would also be a **facultative troglobite**.
trogloxene	An animal that uses caves casually e.g. for temporary shelter, hunting, sleeping, etc... but does not voluntarily spend any extended period of time in them.
ultra-sonic	Any sound frequency that is higher than the maximum that the human ear can normally hear. The normal human hearing range is around 30 Hz - 20 KHz. Bats utilise frequencies of well over 100 KHz
vadose	A vadose passage is one which is formed by a stream with an airspace above it. One way it may have formed is by starting as a phreatic passage, and then becoming vadose as the **water table** dropped.
vertebrates	Animals that contain a vertebral column or backbone.
water table	The level at which the surface of the water is when it is underground.

APPENDIX II — Other Known Caves In Bukit Batu

In addition to the Dark Caves and Temple Cave, a number of other caves are known from Bukit Batu. Some of these are developed caves and are being used for the purpose of religion or tourism while the others are undeveloped (but not entirely undisturbed) caves. It is of course hoped that more caves will be found in the future.

UNDEVELOPED CAVES

Most of these caves were not undiscovered, judging from the amount of graffiti found on their walls, but the Malayan Nature Society Cave Group probably made the first surveys of these caves. They are however not yet published at the time of writing, but it is hoped that this will be done soon. None of these caves are particularly big nor extensive, but a couple of them are quite attractive. None of them, apart from Gua Pandan, contains any significant animal life.

GUA CILI PADI – The MNS-SBCG initially entered this cave by making a precarious climb to an entrance approximately 50 metres up a virtually sheer cliff, because this entrance was easily visible from afar when walking through one of the quarries. A lower, and far more accessible, entrance was discovered not long after. As it turned out, it was well visited by the local residents, and it received its name from the numerous *cili padi* plants (a very small, but devastatingly hot, chili variety enjoyed by many Malaysians) growing near the entrance. They probably got their start from the remains of someone's *nasi lemak*! This cave was also once used by a Malaysian fashion magazine for one of their layouts. It is unlikely to be the same cave that was called Gua Lada by Syers' group. (See **Lost Caves**)

GUA ITCHY (or ICI) BAWAH — Many of the cavers who entered one of the smaller passages of this cave ended up being very itchy all over, probably due to some small particles in the mud. The cave is also directly below Gua Cili Padi, and the two were probably hydrologically connected during their formation – hence *bawah*, which is Malay for "below". The pidgin Malay pun in the name is intended.

GUA PANDAN – This was probably first discovered by Sujauddin Yussof and Neil Nirmal Ariyappala. It is located in a high valley on top of Bukit Batu in a relatively inaccessible location. It requires a scramble up a scree slope from one of the quarries onto Bukit Batu and then down into a valley, followed by a 5 m climb up a slot in a cliff. It contains a reasonably large bat population, but relatively few invertebrates in the guano when compared to the Dark Caves. Due to its high position in the hill, it is the oldest of the known caves in Bukit Batu.

CRYSTAL CAVE – This is a very small cave whose entrance, unusually, is in the ground in secondary, hillside forest rather than a cliff face, not far from Gua Cili

Padi. Most of its walls and floors are covered with crystal growths, some of calcite and others of other minerals. This cave was first discovered by a team from the MNS-SBCG.

SWAMP CAVE – So named because its entrance was in a swamp which came up to the cliff face. Not a very extensive cave.

FIG TREE CAVE – This cave got its name because it's entrance is some distance above ground, and entry was achieved by climbing up the roots of a fig tree that grew in its entrance! Not an extensive cave.

SUJA's CAVE – Only discovered in 1994 by Sujauddin Yussof and others and not yet surveyed, this cave appears to be quite large, with the entrance somewhere above that of the **Ganesh Cave** (see below). Initial explorations suggest that it is mostly vertical in nature, with a drop of around 150 m, as measured by the amount of rope used during the descent of the pitch. It is thought that it might join into the Upper Ganesh Cave.

DEVELOPED CAVES

SMALL DARK CAVE – This is a small ground level cave, and part of it passes beneath the steps up to the Temple Cave. During World War II it was used to store ammunition. It is the first of the art gallery caves encountered after traversing the lake on the raised walkway. See the section on the Temple Caves for more information.

ART GALLERY CAVE – Previously known as the Museum Cave, its development was commissioned in 1972. It is somewhat further west of the Small Dark Cave. The draught felt at the end of this cave is coming from the upper section of the Ganesh Cave. A few potsherds were found in this cave early on its history. See the section on the Temple Caves for more information.

RAMAYANA CAVE – This relatively large cave has a lower and upper section, both of which have accessible entrances. It's ground surface area is not much less than that of the Temple Cave, but the volume is considerably less. The upper section of this cave, also known as the **Upper Ganesh Cave,** is connected to the Art Gallery Cave (see above).

In 1992, this cave had not yet been developed and was called the **GANESH CAVE.** It was however already heavily disturbed, and a large gate had, at some time in the past, been installed across the lower entrance.

The Temple authorities have plans to develop it during 1993, and for that reason it has been included in this section.

SRI AYAPPAN SWAMI TEMPLE – Located some distance around to the east of the Batu Caves area, on the left hand side of the road leading to the Karak Highway from Batu Caves, it is at present somewhat hidden by the multitude of roadside fruit-sellers' stalls. It was developed in the mid-1980's, though worship has taken place there for several decades. It is a well lit, but not very extensive, cave with reasonably large passages and a several entrances. It has some attractive formations, though these have now mostly been modified by the temple's caretakers, one carefully painted to resemble an elephant's head.

The main focus of this temple is not towards Tamils, but Malayalis from Kerala. According to the temple priest, there are only two temples to Lord Ayappan in the world; one in Kerala, and the other in Kuala Lumpur. Devotees and visitors are required to remove their footwear shortly after entering the cave, unlike in the Temple Cave where it is only required in the small courtyard to the main shrine. The main shrine here, dedicated to the Lord Ayappan, is an interesting one; women under the age of 50 are not permitted to worship at it. The reason is because the Lord Ayappan, having descended from heaven, was not born of woman and therefore did not look upon them in the same way as those who had been. Women are also required to conduct their prayers differently at some of the other shrines in this cave. Male worshippers are also required to eat a special diet for 48 days before worshipping at this Ayappan's shrine, and to remove their shirts before entering.

In true, democratic, Hindu fashion however, this temple is not averse to catering to the local population. Shrines to Ganesh and Muruga, among others, are present in the cave, and a shrine containing a *vel* is just outside the entrance to the cave and another one is inside.

The guano of a small remnant bat population, can be seen and felt (by compulsorily bare feet), sprinkled across most of the concreted floor of the cave.

The Sri Ayappan Swami Temple is not associated with the Sri Subramania Swamy Temple in any way apart from the fact that they are both Hindu Temples.

LOST CAVES

Several caves have been recorded in the past which no longer exist, in all likelihood due to quarrying. A couple of others, described by the original explorers, have not been identified from their descriptions, though they may still exist.

Hornaday and Daly originally described three caves; Gua Belah (Split Cave), Gua Lada (Chili Cave), and Gua Lambong (Hanging Cave). Gua Lambong appears to have been what is now the Temple Cave, and which Ridley called the Cathedral Cave. The inset in the section on History discusses another, interesting, difference in the original descriptions of the cave.

Dover referred to "numerous" smaller caves (other than the Dark Caves) but gave no details by which they might be identified.

Apart from the Dark Caves and and the Cathedral (Temple) Cave, Ridley also explored three other caves: Quarry Cave, Sakai Cave, and Fallen Cave. None of these can be found today and they have probably been destroyed together with many, if not all, of Dover's "numerous" caves. Some of these caves might have been of archaeological value, had they survived.

APPENDIX III — Bibliography And Additional Reading List

Abraham, H.C. (1923). **A new spider of the genus *Liphistius*.** *J. Malay. Br. Roy. Asiatic Soc.* 13

Annandale, N., Brown, J.C., & Gravely, F.H. (1913). **The limestone caves of Burma and the Malay Peninsula.** *J. Asiatic Soc. Bengal.* 9:391-423

Aw, P.C. (1978). **Conservation of limestone hills – a geologist's view.** *Malay. Nat. J.* 30(3/4):449-459

Brook, D.B. & Waltham, A.C. (Eds.) (1979). *Caves of Mulu.* The Royal Geographical Society, London. 52 pp.

Bristowe, W.S. (1952). **The arachnid fauna of the Batu Caves in Malaya.** *An. Mag. Nat. Hist. Ser.* 5:697-707

Bullock, J.A. (1963). **Notes on the cave fauna of two limestone massifs in Taman Negara.** *Malay. Nat. J.* 17:46-52

Bullock, J.A. (1971). **Fauna of Gua Anak Takun.** *Malay. Nat. J.* 24:95-97

Bullock, J.A. (1972). **Cave biology in Malaysia.** *Malay. Nat. J.* 25:135-141

Cahill, T. & Nicolls, M. (1991). **Charting the splendors of Lechuguilla Cave.** *National Geographic* 179(3):34-59

Chin, S.C. (1977). **The limestone flora of Malaya 1.** *Gards' Bull. Singapore* 30:165-219

Chin, S.C. (1979). **The limestone flora of Malaya 2.** *Gards' Bull. Singapore* 32:64-203

Chin, S.C. (1983a). **The limestone flora of Malaya 3.** *Gards' Bull. Singapore* 35:137-190

Chin, S.C. (1983b). **The limestone flora of Malaya 4.** *Gards' Bull. Singapore* 36:31-91

Colless, D.H. (1962). ***Chetoneura cavernae*, n. gen., n. sp. from Batu Caves, Malaya.** *Pacific Ins.* 4(2):437-39

Cottarelli, V. and Mura, G. (1982). ***Parastenocaris arganoi* n. sp., a new Troglobian species from Malaysia.** *Malay. Nat. J.* 35:65-71

Crowther, J. (1978). **Karst regions and caves of the Malay Peninsula, west of the Main Range.** *Trans. Brit. Cave Res. Ass.* 5(4):199-214

Crowther, J. (1978). **The Gunong Gajah-Tempurong massif, Perak, and its associated cave system, Gua Tempurong.** *Malay. Nat. J.* 32(1):1-17

Crowther, J. (1986). **Karst environments and ecosystems in Peninsular Malaysia.** *Malay. Nat. J.* 39:231-257

Daly, D.D. (1879). **Caves at Sungei Batu in Selangor.** *J. Straits Bt. Roy. As. Soc.* 3:116-119

Davison, G.W.H., Kishokumar, J., & Wan Abdul Latif Wan Jafar (1991). **Ipoh limestone - the next step.** *Malayan Naturalist.* 44(2&3):29-31

DeHarveng, and LeClerc, P. (1989). **Recherches sure les faunes cavernicoles d'Asie due sud-est.** *Mémoires de Biospéologie. 16:91-110*

Dover, C. (1928). **The fauna of the Batu Caves.** *The Malayan Naturalist 2(1):35-38* (The Singapore Natural History Society)

Dover, C. (Ed) (1929). **Fauna of the Batu Caves, Selangor.** *J. Fed. Malay States Mus.* 14:325-91

Eavis, A.J. (Ed.) (1981). *Caves of Mulu '80.* The Royal Geographical Society, London. 52 pp.

Eavis, A.J. (Ed.) (1985). *Caves of Mulu '84.* British Cave Research Association, Bridgwater, U.K. 56 pp.

Freeman, P. (1962). **Chironomidae from the Batu Caves, Malaya (Diptera: Nematocera).** *Pacific Ins.* 4(1):129-31

Gale, S.J.(1986) **The hydrological development of tropical tower karst: an example from Peninsular Malaysia.** in *New Directions in Karst* (Paterson, K. and Sweeting, M.M. eds.) Geo Books, Norwich.

Henderson, M.R. (1939). **The flora of the limestone hills of the Malay Peninsula.** *J. Mal. Br. Roya. As. Soc.* 17:13-87

Holland, Eric G. (1955). *A guide to Batu Caves.* Singapore 15 pp

Hornaday, W.T. (1885). *Two years in the jungle.* London: Kegan Paul, Trench

Kawakatsu, M., Mitchell, R.W., Oki, I., Tamura, S., Yussof, S. (1989). **Taxonomic and karyological studies of *Dugesia batuensis* BALL, 1970 (Turbellaria, Tricladida, Paludicola), from the Batu Caves, Malaysia.** *J. Speleol. Soc. Japan.* 14:1-14

Kiew B. H. (1979). **A note on the frogs and toads of Batu Caves.** *Malay. Nat. J.* 33(1):67-69

Kiew, B. H. (1987). **Exploring the Limestone Hills of Kenyir, Terengganu.** *Nature Malaysiana* 12(2):28-31

Kiew, R. (1991). **Chapter 6 - The Limestone Flora.** in *The state of nature conservation in Malaysia.* Kiew, R. (Ed.) Malayan Nature Society 238pp

Lyon, B. (1983). *Venturing Underground - the new speleo's guide.* E.P. Publishing Limited, Bradford Road, East Ardsley, Wakefield, West Yorkshire, WF3 2JN, England.

Matthews, J.M. (1961). **Cave archaeology in Malaya.** In Wyatt-Smith, J., & Wycherley, P.R., (Eds), *Nature Conservation in Western Malaysia.* pp 79-82. Malayan Nature Society, Kuala Lumpur

McClure H.E. (1961). **Batu Caves, Kuala Lumpur.** In Wyatt-Smith, J., & Wycherley, P.R., (Eds), *Nature Conservation in Western Malaysia. Malayan Nature Journal* Anniversay Issue pp 73-78.

McClure, H.E., Boo Liat Lim, Winn, S.E. (1967). **Fauna of the Dark Cave, Batu Caves, Kuala Lumpur, Malaysia.** *Pacific Insects* 9(3):399-428

Medway, Lord. (1977). **The lost caves at Batu, Selangor.** *Malay. Nat. J.* 30(1):87-91

Meredith, M. & Martinez, D. (1986). *Vertical Caving.* Lyon Equipment, Dent, Dedberch, Cumbria, UK. 80 pp

Malayan Nature Society (1965). *Malayan Nature Journal.* Malaysian Caves Issue. 19(1):1-112

Malayan Nature Society (1980). *The Malayan Naturalist.* Batu Caves Issue. 34(1&2):1-22

49

Malayan Nature Society (1990). *A conservation assessment of limestone hills in the Kinta Valley. Final Report.* Unpublished report. 202 pp

Malayan Nature Society (1991). *Management proposals for the Dark Caves and associated caves at Batu Caves.* Submitted to the Selangor State Government. 51pp

Meredith, M., Wooldridge, J., Lyon, B. (1992). *Giant Caves of Borneo.* Tropical Press Sdn. Bhd., Kuala Lumpur. 142 pp

MNS Selangor Branch Caving Group (1984). **The caves at Batu Luas.** *Malayan Naturalist* 38(2):25-28

MNS Selangor Branch Caving Group (1985). **Report of the Selangor Branch Caving Group Batu Kepayang 1984 Expedition, Taman Negara.** *Malayan Naturalist* 38(3):2-44

Molesworth-Allen, B. (1961). **Limestone hills near Ipoh.** In Wyatt-Smith, J., & Wycherley, P.R., (Eds), *Nature Conservation in Western Malaysia.* pp 68-72. Malayan Nature Society, Kuala Lumpur

Montgomery, N.R. (1982). *Single Rope Techniques - a guide for vertical cavers* Sydney Speleological Society Occasional Paper No.7, Sydney Speleological Society, P.O. Box 198, Broadway, NSW, Australia. 123 pp

Moore, G.W., & Sullivan, G.N. (1978). *Speleology : the study of caves.* Zephyrus Press, New Jersey

Ng, S.M. (1974). **The biology of *Pycnoscelus striatus* Kirby, the cave roach, with special reference to nymphal development and instar differentiation.** *Malay. Nat. J.* 28(2):84-89

Platnick, N.I. and Sedgwick, W.C. (1984). **A revision of the spider genus *Liphistius* (Araneae, Mesothelae).** *American Museum Novitates* 2781:1-31

Price, L. (1992).**The Batu Caves, Kuala Lumpur, Selangor, Western Malaysia.** *The International Caver (3):24-26*

Quate. L.W. (1962). **The psychodidae of Batu Caves, Malaya (Diptera).** *Pacific Ins.* 4(1):219-314

Ridley, H.N. (1898). **On the caves in the Malay Peninsula.** *Rep. Brit. Assoc. Advancement of Science, Bristol meeting 1898.* pp 572-582

Ridley, H.N. (1898). **The white snake of the Selangor Caves.** *J. Straits Br. Roy. Asiatic Soc.* 31:99-101

Smart, P.L. & Willis, R.G. (*Eds.*). (1982). **Mulu '80 Expedition.** *Trans. Brit. Cave Res. Ass.* Vol.9(2):55-164 (Entire volume)

Soepadmo, E. & Ho T.H. (*Eds.*). (1971). *A Guide to Batu Caves.* Jointly published by the Malayan Nature Society & the Batu Caves Protection Association. Kuala Lumpur.

Tan, K.H. (1970). **Reproduction of the cave roach *Pycnoscelus striatus*.** *Malay. Nat. J.* 23:168-170

Thornton, I.W. (1962). **Psocids (Psocoptera) from the Batu Caves, Malaya.** *Pacific Ins.* 4(2):441-55

Tunku Mohd Nazim Yaacob (1991). **Chapter 2 - Caves.** in *The State Of Nature Conservation In Malaysia.* Kiew, R. (Ed.) Malayan Nature Society 238pp

Valli, E. & Summers, D. (1990). **Nest gatherers of the Tiger Cave.** *National Geographic* 177(1):107-133

Wells, D. R. & Labang, D. (1974). **Cave earwigs transported by a fruit bat.** Note. *Malay. Nat. J.* 27:59

Werner, F.G. (1962). **The Aderidae of the Batu Caves, Malaya (Coleoptera).** *Pacific Ins.* 4(1):121-27

Wilford, G.E. (1963). **Limestone cave formation in Sarawak and North Borneo.** in Proceedings of the British Borneo Geological Conference 1961 *Brit. Borneo Geol. Surv. Bull* 4:161-173

Wilford, G.E. (1964). *The Geology of Sarawak and Sabah Caves.* Geological Survey, Borneo Region Bulletin 6. 181 pp

Wyatt-Smith, J. (1960). **Dusky leaf monkeys at Batu Caves.** (Letter). *Malay. Nat. J.* 14:225-226

Wycherley, P.R. (1972). **Ridley and Batu Caves.** *Malay. Nat. J.* 25:22-37

Yussof, S. (1985). **The caves of Anak Bukit Takun.** *Nature Malaysiana* 10(4):4-9

Yussof, S. (1987). **Gua Anak Takun revisited.** *Malayan Naturalist* 40(3&4):12-16

Yussof, S. (1988). **Some invertebrates from Batu Caves.** *Nature Malaysiana* 13(2):24-31

Yussof, S. (1990). **The role of Taman Negara in orchid conservation.** *J. of Wildlife and Parks* Special Taman Negara Golden Jubilee issue. 10:25-29

INDEX

aborigines, 6, 7
  Besisi, 6
  Sakai, 6
Achatina fulica, see *snails, giant African*
albinism, albino, 29
Anak Bukit Takun, 10
Annandale, 12
ants, 37
Archaeology, 5
Arixenia, see *earwig*
Art Gallery Cave, see *caves, Art Gallery*
assassin bugs, 37

Bagauda, 37
balsams (Impatiens spp.), 23
bats, 4, 5, 11, 25, 26, 27, 29, 30, 31, 33, 37, 47, 48, 49
  and durian, 30
  and mangroves, 30
  and pollination, 30
  and snakes, 32
  and swiftlets, 31
  bones, 5
  Cave,Diadem Horseshoe (Hipposideros diadema), 29
  Cave,Dog Faced (Eonycteris spelaea), 29
  destruction of fruit, 31
  flying foxes (Vampyrus), 31
  frugivorous, 25, 26, 30
  insectivorous, 26, 30
  largest group of mammals, 30
  naked,(Cheiromeles torquatus), 28
  seed dispersal, 31
  sonar, 30
  trogloxenes, 27
  vampire, 31
Batu Caves Protection Association, 7
Beccari, Odoardo, 12, 21
Begonia phoeniogramma, 23
begonias, 23
blasting, 8, 22
bones
  bats, 5
  monkeys, 6
Bristowe, 12

British Colonial Office, 7
Brown, 12
Bufo asper, see *toads*
Bufo melanostictus, see *toads*
Bukit Batu, 1, 3, 4, 5, 9, 11, 13, 14, 15, 21, 22, 23, 24, 38, 50, 51

calcite, 17, 18, 19, 20, 21, 46, 47, 49
calcium carbonate, 14, 17, 46, 47
Capricornis sumatraensis, 48, see also *serau*
case moths, 37
Cathedral Cave, see *Temple Cave*
cave drawings, 6
cave ecology, 25
cave racer, 29
caves
  Art Gallery, 1, 3, 5, 15, 41, 51, 52
  Batu, 31
  Cathedral, 38
  Clear Water, in Mulu N.P., 15
  Dark, 1, 3, 4, 5, 7, 8, 9, 10, 11, 12, 15, 16, 22, 25, 26, 27, 29, 32, 33, 34, 35, 37, 38, 46, 50, 51, 53
  deepest, 15
  Deer, in Mulu N.P., 15
  Gua Anak Daun Menari (Taman Negara), 27
  Gua Cili Padi, 50
  Gua Cintamanis(near Karak), 27
  Gua Daun Menari (Taman Negara), 27
  Gua Lambong, 4, 6, 38
  Gua Lipas (Raub), 27
  Ici Bawah, 15
  longest, 15
  Lower Ganesh, 15
  Lubang Nasib Bagus, Mulu N.P., 31
  Mammoth Cave/Flint Ridge, longest cave system, 15
  Niah, 28, 31
  Sarawak Chamber, largest, 15
  Small Dark, 1, 3, 15, 41, 51
  Swinging, 4
  Temple, 1, 3, 4, 5, 6, 7, 11, 14, 15, 16, 20, 24, 38, 40, 41, 42, 43, 50, 51, 52, 53
  Tiger, 31

centipede
    cave, 27, 28, 34, 36
    Scutigera, 27, 28, 34, 35, 36
Cheiromeles torquatus, see *bats, naked*
Chinese farmers, 4, 7
Chirita, 23
cockroach, 34
    cave, 9, 10, 11, 35
    house, 10, 35
conservation, 7, 8, 9, 22, 23, 24, 35, 37
corrasion, 13, 46
corrosion, 13, 46
cricket
    cave, (Diestrammena gravelyi), 12, 28, 29, 36
    mole (Gryllotalpa fulvipes), 37

Daly, D.D., 4, 6, 11, 18, 38
Dark Caves, see *caves, Dark*
deities, 38
Devonian/Carboniferous, 13
Diestrammena gravelyi, see *cricket, cave*
Doratodesmus, see *millipedes*
Dover, C., 12, 22
Dugesia batuensis, 36, see also *planarian*
durian and bats, 30
dynamite, 5

earwig
    Arixenia esau, 28
Echinodorus ridleyi, 10
echo-location
    bats, 30
    Blue Whistling Thrush, 32
    swiftlets, 31
ecology, 1, 12, 21, 22, 24, 25, 28, 33
    bats involvement in, 30
    cave, 25
    limestone, 22
Elaphe taeniura, 29, see *snakes, cave racer*
energy
    cosmic, 40
    expenditure, 29
    flowchart, 25
    guano as a source of,, 25
    sunlight, 25
Eonycteris spelaea, see *bats*
Europeans, 4, 7

fireflies, 37
Flying foxes, 31
formations, 16
    cave flowers, 21
    cave pearls, 21
    cave straws, 20
    column, 19
    curtains, 20
    draperies, 20
    flow-stone, 20
    gour pools, 20
    gypsum flowers, 21
    helictites, 21
    rimstone dams, 20
    shawls, 20
    stalactite, 16, 18, 19, 48, 49
    stalagmite, 8, 9, 16, 18, 19, 49
fossils, 5, 22, 35
frogs, 22, 24
frugivorous, 47
fungus-gnat, 37

gesneriads, 23
Glyphiulius, see *millipede*
graffiti, 9, 50
Gravely, 12
Gryllotalpa, see *cricket*
Gua Anak Bukit Takun, 10
Gua Lambong, see *caves, Gua Lambong*
guano, 1, 4, 10, 22, 25, 26, 27, 31, 34, 36, 37, 47, 51, 52
    as a source of energy, 25
    mining, 4, 6, 7, 11, 26

Hanging Cave, see *caves, Swinging*
Heynes-Wood, M., 12
Hindu, 38, 39
Hinduism, 39
    history of, 39
Hipposideros diadema, see *bats*
Hornaday, William T, 4, 6, 11, 38

Ice caves, 13
Imperata cylindrica, 22
invertebrates, 10, 12, 22, 25, 26, 27, 33, 34, 36, 37, 47
    population, 26
Islam

succeeding Hinduism, 39

kambing gurun, 24, 47, 48
kavadi, 42, 43, 44, 47
Kuala Lumpur, vii, 1, 3, 13, 14, 21, 38, 41, 43, 48, 52

L. batuensis, see *spider*
lallang, 22
Langkawi, 11, 23
Lava caves, 12
limestone ecology, 22
limestone flora, 22
limestone funa, 24
Liphistius, see *spider, Liphistius batuensis*

Macaca fascicularis, see *monkeys*
Macaranga, 22
Mahabharata, 40
Malayan Nature Society, 1, 7, 8, 9, 50
Maxburettia rupicola, 23, 28
Maxburretia rupicola, 11
McClure, E., 12, 25, 32, 34
millipede
    Doratodesmus, 37
millipede;Glyphiulius, 37
mites, 37
MNS, see *Malayan Nature Society*
monkeys
    banded leaf, 24
    bones, 6
    dusky leaf, 24
    long tailed macaque, 24
monkeys;long-tailed macaques, 39
Monophyllaea, 23
mosquitoes, 34
moths, 34
Mulu National Park, 15, 20
Murugan, 42, 43, 45
Museum Cave, see *caves, Art Gallery*
Myophonus caeruleus, see *thrush, blue whistling*

nectivorous, 47

Opeas, see *snails*
orchids, 23
    Bulbophyllum, 23
    Calanthe vestita, 23

Coelogyne, 23
Eria, 23
Paphiopedilum, 23
    niveum, 23

P. americana, see *cockroach, house*
Pandanus calcicola, 23
Parabathynella malayana, 37
Paraboea, 23
Periplaneta, , see *cockroach, house*
pigmentation, 29
Piper, 22
pisolites, 21, 48
planarian (Dugesia batuensis), 11, 36
Presbytis melalophus, see *monkeys*
Presbytis obscurus, see *monkeys*
Pycnoscelus, see *cockroach, cave*

railway, funicular, 38
Ranalisma rostrata, 10
rats, 33
Reseau Jean Bernard, deepest cave, 15
Ridley, H. N., 4, 5, 6, 10, 11, 22, 23, 24, 32, 33, 36, 38
rockfalls, 8
rubbish, 9

Sandstone caves, 13
Sarax, , see *Scorpion, tailless whip*
SBCG, see *Selangor Branch Cave Group*
scorpion, 33, 36, 46
    tailless whip (Sarax brachydactylus), 28, 36, 46
sedimentation, 13
Selangor Branch Cave Group, 1, 8, 9, 50, 51
Selangor State Government, 8, 9
serau, 11, 24, 47, 48
shrews, 33
Silurian, 13
Small Dark Cave, see *caves, Small Dark*
snails, 24, 32, 34
    giant African (Achatina fulica), 32
    Opeas, 37
    shell heaps, 32
snakes, 32
    cave racer (Elaphe taeniura), 32
    python, 32
solution, 13

sonar, 30, see also e*cho location*, 46
speleologist, 46
speleothem, 17
spider
    huntsman, 37
    Liphistius batuensis, 9, 10, 28, 35, 36
Sri Maha Mariamman, 38, 43
Sri Subramania Swamy, 38, 52
stalactites, see *formations*
stalagmites, see *formations*
swiftlets, 25, 26, 31, 47
    trogloxenes, 27
Swinging Cave, see *caves, Swinging*
Syers, H. C., 4, 11, 50
symbiosis, 49

Temple Cave, see *caves, Temple*
Templer Park, 10
temples
    Ganesha, 40
    Sri Subramania Swamy, 40
    Vali Devayanai, 41
Thaipusam, 1, 5, 41, 42, 43, 44, 47, 49
Thambusamy Pillay, 38
thrush, blue whistling (Myophonus
       caeruleus), 32
ticks, 37
toads, 24, 33
    Bufo asper, 33
    Bufo melanostictus, 33
Triassic, 13
troglobites, 27
troglophiles, 27
trogloxenes, 27, 29

worms, 34

PLATE 1 : The entrance to the Dark Caves was never really worth photographing while the gate and the mock stalagmites were there. Since they were removed by the MNS-SBCG, the view has become a most attractive one.

PLATE 2 : This magnificent flowstone in Cavern B is particularly attractive sometime after heavy rain, when water ripples and flows down over its surface as a shiny film.

PLATE 3 : This attractive stalagmite is located in a short offshoot chamber to Cavern D. The sharp detail on its decorations indicate that it was formed after the second time the river flowed through. (See page 13 in the main text).

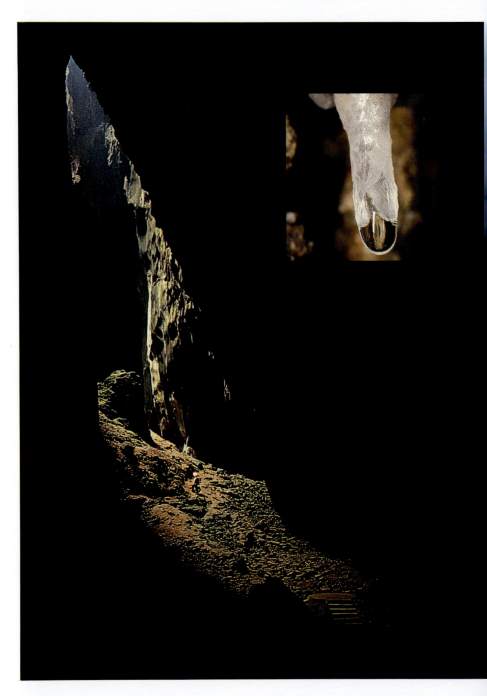

PLATE 4 : The view from the walkway in the Dark Caves, looking towards the skylight in the Great Cavern can be spectacular. It varies with the season and the time of day.

INSET : A cave straw, with a drop of water about to fall off. Note the thin, crystalline structure of the straw walls.

PLATE 5 : This aerial view of Batu Caves clearly shows the devastation wreaked by the quarrying. It also very clearly shows the large, deep erosion pits (dolines) all over the surface of the hill.

PLATE 6: This splendid view of the typical dense Malayan limestone surface vegetation, interspersed with large *Pandanus calcicolus* plants, belies the dangerously sharp, rain eroded, and slippery limestone pinnacles that cover the surface of the hill.

PLATE 7 : Due to the size of Cavern C, many of its large features cannot usually be seen all at once, since it is not easy to provide sufficient light. Taking multiple-flash photographs is the usual way of overcoming this problem. Even so, the success or failure of such an effort is often a question of trial and error. The silhouettes in this photo are all of the same person, who changed position

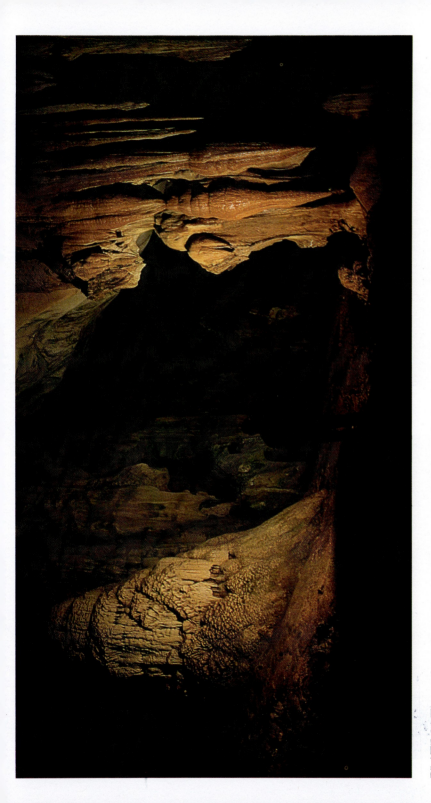

PLATE 8: The stalagmite on the left has been eroded through the river's resurgence in the cave, whereas the elaborate column on the right is still in the process of being formed, as can be deduced from its glistening surface. These formations are found towards the end of Cavern C.

PLATE 10 : Dry limestone looks very different from wet limestone, as can be seen from the lower half of this photo. This speleothem is often called "The Jellyfish and Squid" due to the appearance of the formations.

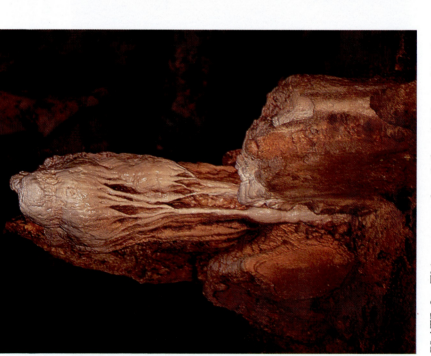

PLATE 9 : This spectacular, 1.5 m high, stalagmite illustrates very well the colour differences that can occur in speleothem due to impurities collected by water seeping through the limestone.

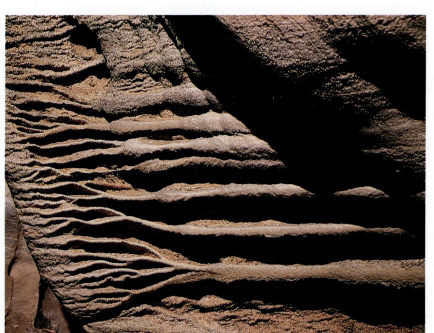

PLATE 12 : Nature repeats its patterns in the most unusual places. This flowstone found in the Great Chamber resembles an aerial view of hill erosion patterns or a river estuary.

PLATE 11 : This striking combination of stalagmite, stalactite, and flowstone are found high in the ceiling of a side passage of Cavern D in the Dark Caves.

PLATE 13 : The main chamber of the Crystal Cave is not very big. It does however display the classic features that make a cave instantly recognisable as such i.e. stalagmites and stalagtites in silhouette. The light source for this photo was a caver's carbide headlamp, and the photo required a time exposure of approximately 30 seconds.

PLATE 15 : If these crystals from Crystal Cave had grown in any other accessible cave in Malaysia, they would have been long gone. Crystal Cave is however relatively difficult to find, which has kept these crystals pristine.

PLATE 14 : The crystal in these 5-10 cm wide rosettes, found in Crystal Cave, appear to grow from the centre of the rosette. New crystals point inwards at first, and the pressure subsequent ones cause them to rotate outwards.

PLATE 17 : This clean and white formation is another rarity for the same reason as the one in Plate 16. It is found in the passages at the bottom of the Pothole Chamber.

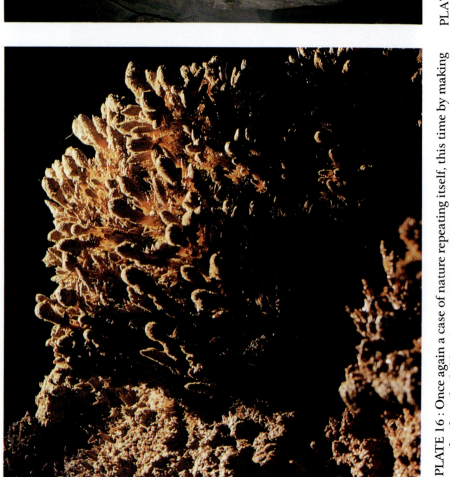

PLATE 16 : Once again a case of nature repeating itself, this time by making a speleothem look like the coral from which the limestone was originally formed. Decorations such as this one are quite uncommon in Malaysia due to vandalism. This one was found in Crystal Cave.

PLATE 18 : The paler, cavernicole, form of *Elaphe taeniura* makes use of even the smallest irregularities on the surface to climb cave walls.

PLATE 19 : If water runs down both the inside and the outside of a cave straw, the straw can eventually become a stalactite by thickening around the outside, as is happening to the ones in this picture.

PLATE 20 : Bats are generally not easy to see close-up in the Dark Caves since they roost high up on the cave walls. The only time one can see them is when they are sick, have fallen to the ground, and no longer have the strength to fly back up, such as with these two here. Usually all that can be seen are the bones lying on the ground. On the left is the endearing, frugivorous, Cave Fruit-bat (*Eonycteris spelaea*) and the other is the insectivorous Diadem Horseshoe Bat (*Hipposideros diadema*).

PLATE 21 : The nest of the rare trapdoor spider, *Liphistius batuensis*, can be found on the walls of Selangor caves. The trip lines radiating from the main trapdoor make the nest itself look very much like a strange spider

PLATE 22 : The *Liphistius* spider waits at the entrance of its funnel, hiding beneath the trapdoor, with one leg placed more or less between each pair of trip lines. When potential prey trips a line, the spider knows which way to jump.

PLATE 23 : The *Liphistius* spider is one of the favourite foods of the cave centipede, *Scutigera decipiens*. The increase in their population over recent years could have been one of the contributing factors in the decline of the Batu Caves *Liphistius* population.

PLATE 24 : Mating in *Scutigera* consists of a slow, wary, approach followed by the male handing over a small bag of sperm to the female, which she then inserts inside herself to fertilise her eggs.

PLATE 25 : *Damarchus cavernicolus* is another trapdoor spider found in the Dark Caves. It is most common at the end of Cavern C. Patient observers will be able to watch them pop in and out of their tubes to catch prey.

PLATE 26 : This spider, probably a psechrid, is not a trapdoor spider. It makes a conspicuous web, and carries its eggcase. Note, both in this spider, and the one above, the lack of pseudo-segments.

PLATE 27: This fearsome-looking tailless whip scorpion, *Sarax brachydactylus*, is one of the largest arachnids (spider relatives) found in caves. It can have a "feeler span" of over 30 cm.

PLATE 28 By contrast, the pseudo-scorpion *Dhanus* sp. (another arachnid) is one of the smaller ones found in the caves (Mites are much smaller). Half a dozen of these mites or pseudo-scorpions could easily fit on the nail of one's little finger!

PLATE 29 : The light-shy cave cockroach, *Pycnoscelus striatus*, is becoming harder to photograph as its population in the Batu Caves declines from year to year. See the section on Specific Conservation Notes for more information.

PLATE 30 : The common house cockroach, *Periplaneta americana*, is taking over Cavern A, where before the 1970's years ago the cave cockroach held sway. The house cockroach occurs in the tens of thousands in the Cavern A, all over the walls and floor of the cave.

PLATE 31 : The female cave cricket, *Diestrammena gravelyi*, has a horn-shaped appendage, known as an ovipositor, at the base of her abdomen. This is used to place eggs in the ground or guano.

PLATE 32 : Many casual cave visitors have speculated that the white cockroaches they sometimes see are cave adapted. This photo of a normal cockroach instar moulting should put an end to such speculations.

PLATE 33 : The long legged assassin bug, *Bagauda lucifuga*, sneaks up to its prey, grabs it with its mantis-like forelegs, and literally sucks the juices out of the hapless victim.

PLATE 34 : At certain times of the year, the black earwig. *Chelisoches morio*, is quite common at the bend that connects Cavern A and B. The earwig is sometimes also heavily parasitised by a species of mite.

PLATE 35 : This very light-coloured species of snail *(Opeas sp.)*, up to 2 cm long, might be a cave adapted species since it doesn't react to light. It lives in the thousands in the guano-rich drip stream in Cavern C.

PLATE 36 : The planarian, *Dugesia batuensis*, was until recently thought to be a cave adapted species, but it has since been found on the outside. It is however still most common inside the Dark Caves, especially in Cavern C.

PLATE 37 : *Glyphiulius* sp. is the most commonly found cave millipede, and is most abundant near the end of Cavern C. It scavenges on dead bats, invertebrates, and guano. It might also eat fungus growing on the guano, but this is not known for sure.

PLATE 38 : Since it does not react to light, it has been suggested that this *Doratodesmus* sp. millipede is a troglobyte. from some angles it looks somewhat like a section of a mammalian backbone.

PLATE 39 : The gesneriad *Chirita caliginosa* is quite common around Batu Caves. It is one of the many gesneriads found on limestone. It is a relative of several house plants, including the African violet and the *Gloxinia*.

PLATE 40 : The fan palm *Maxburretia rupicola* is a rare endemic palm, and it is found only on the three Selangor limestone hills. It is just one of several endemic plants found on Bukit Batu. Its nearest relative is on the northern island of Langkawi.

PLATE 41 : The Temple Cave, on an ordinary day, is simply awe-inspiring, and not just to the first time visitor. The impression it makes is almost beyond description and it is easy to understand why it was chosen as a place for worship in the first place.

PLATE 42 : During the festival of Thaipusam, the awe one would normally feel due to the size of the cave is completely overwhelmed by the crowd, the riot of colours, and the smell of camphor, coconut, and bodies.

PLATE 43 : The Vali Devayanai Temple at the bottom of the Temple Cave shaft is in quite a spectacular location.

PLATE 44 : On normal days the 272 steps leading up to the cave are virtually empty, but during Thaipusam the people literally flow UP the stairs. In recent years it has been less crowded due to better management.

PLATE 46 : The fruit need not always be lime, as they are in this case. Oranges are also quite commonly used. They simply serve to provide a little weight to the hooks in order to emphasise the devotee's sincerity.

PLATE 45 : The kavadi is often very heavy and the devotee may need some assistance carrying it. Note the careful placement of the hooks and chains to produce an attractive pattern.